D0690505
The Art of
Sooke Harbour House

Dedication

To my mother Charlotte,
for her love of art

A portion of the proceeds
from the sale of this book
will be donated to
the Art Department
of Sooke's Edward Milne Community School.

The Art of Sooke Harbour House

FEATURING

Recipes inspired by the Art

Frédérique Philip

Sooke Harbour House

The Art of Sooke Harbour House
Featuring Recipes Inspired by the Art

First published in Canada in 2003 by Sooke Harbour House.

ISBN 0-9732788-0-3

For bulk purchases of this book or to gain more information about the art featured within, which is for sale, please contact:

Sooke Harbour House, Publisher
1528 Whiffen Spit Road, Sooke, British Columbia
Canada V0S 1N0
Ph. 250.642.3421 Fax: 250.642.6988
E-mail: gallery@sookeharbourhouse.com
Website: www.sookeharbourhouse.com

Creative Director:	J. Scott
Cover concept:	Cameron Craig
Book design:	Miriam MacPhail
Lettering art:	Jasmine Philip
Photography:	Andrei Fedorov
Editor and writer:	Lynne Mustard
Scanning and Pre-press:	Island Graphics, Victoria, B.C.

Printed and bound in Canada by Generation Printing, Vancouver, B. C.

Acknowledgments

The guest rooms, hallways, foyer, study, dining room...
in fact every nook and cranny
of Sooke Harbour House Restaurant and Inn...
are radiant with local art and craftsmanship.

View of Dining Room,
Sooke Harbour House

Therefore, this book was conceived two years ago as an art catalogue, to promote many of the local artists I have had the privilege of knowing. The concept evolved, with the collaboration of photographer extraordinaire Andrei Fedorov, diligent organizer J. Scott, book designer Miriam MacPhail, editor and writer Lynne Mustard, our head chef Edward Tuson, my enthusiastic assistant Chloé Lemire-Elmore, our four artistic children: Benjamin, Jasmine, Nishka and Rissa, and the quiet support of Sinclair. Along with all the talented artists featured, we started another creative process that reflects our lives at the Sooke Harbour House. This process will illustrate how food, art and gardens are all connected and how, together, they are an expression of life.

I wish you much enjoyment while exploring this book, cooking with our recipes, and appreciating the local artists who have nourished my own inspiration. We look forward to presenting the art to you in all its different forms when you visit, dine with us and meet our large family of artists.

Frédérique PH

Frederique Philip

Sooke Harbour House
on Whiffen Spit Beach

CONTENTS

FOREWORD

Art has always been with our species,
ever since we could call ourselves human.
To embellish, brighten or add a bit of grace...whether it's simply
a beaded necklace, a design on a canoe paddle or a molding around
a doorway...may be the essence of what it is to be human.

Robert Bateman

PHOTO OF ROBERT BATEMAN: BIRGIT FREYBE BATEMAN

Portia, when referring to the quality of mercy in Shakespeare's *The Merchant of Venice*, said "...it droppeth as the gentle rain from heaven upon the earth beneath. It is twice blest; *it blesseth him that gives and him that takes.*"

And that's what art does. In my case, I think in every case, it blesses the artist the most. You create something with your own hands that never existed before in the history of the planet. In a sense, we can broaden the definition of art as far as we want, to include even a dish that is beautifully prepared and brought to the table. (The recipes included in this book were inspired by the art!) And I am in complete agreement with Frederique Philip, that it's important for everyone to create, even if you believe you aren't talented in any particular way. It can be anything...a lovely piece of creative knitting or even a bit of a garden. Some gardens are more creative than many paintings.

In British Columbia, we are blessed with a great number of artists. The works of several are presented here; I'm sure you will enjoy paging through and discovering which are your favourites.

We're also blessed with people who are interested in employing artists. The patronage that Frederique and Sinclair Philip have so generously provided local artists is exemplary. In fact, everything about Sooke Harbour House is wonderful from beginning to end: the setting, the artful décor, the food, the views. It has this wholesome, "small is beautiful" ambiance that I really like, along with a very civilized feeling that you often get in Europe, where there is a more integrated, holistic approach to living.

Canadians should look around the world for other ideas. Holland, for example, has created a beautiful blend of art, nature and business in its communities. We Canadians tend to be too pigeon-holed in our approach: "this is art", "that is building" and "that is jobs". We don't tend to have that integrated, holistic approach. There could be more environmental and artistic sensibility in the way we live and work. In this regard, I think Sooke Harbour House is showing the way. So too is the town of

Chemainus, with its murals. Art and esthetics are extremely important to the economy. I admire the public-spirited people who revitalized Chemainus and are now seeding a "West Coast renaissance" with the Arts and Cultural Accord Foundation.

Increasingly we're living in a packaged world...the instant pudding world...that's designed and packaged by some corporation somewhere. Things are slick and smooth and sweet and convenient and all you do is put down your credit card and buy the package. It isn't one of a kind; it isn't hand-done; it isn't special. Shoddy mass production, consumerism and "progress" are having devastating effects on the planet.

By focusing on "the artful celebration of life", Frederique and her family, and this book, set a good example of how it can be done better.

Robert Bateman

Robert Bateman
Blue Heron

An Unconventional Art Gallery

The Gallery at Sooke Harbour House entices guests and visitors to discover the art collection located throughout the Inn's public areas and grounds.

The purpose of this book is to highlight the Gallery and provide a sampling of the art included in the on-going and ever-changing exhibitions at Sooke Harbour House.

The artists featured in this book exhibit at the Sooke Harbour House Gallery and all the work shown is for sale. For prices or commissions, contact the artists directly through the information provided in this catalogue, or through the Sooke Harbour House Gallery at 250 642-3421, e-mail gallery@sookeharbourhouse.com.

THE SPECTACULAR BEAUTY OF THE PACIFIC NORTHWEST is a powerful magnet for both artists and visitors from around the world. Many of those visitors travel to Sooke on the southern tip of scenic Vancouver Island, just west of the city of Victoria, to stay at Sooke Harbour House.

The elegant country auberge has many attractions. In addition to being "one of the five best Country Inns in the world," (*Gourmet Magazine*, 2000), and chosen as "one of the Top Ten Inns in the world", (*Travel and Leisure* magazine, 2002), Sooke Harbour House is also a highly unconventional art gallery.

Guests and visitors at Sooke Harbour House enjoy the fresh, regional cuisine of a five-star restaurant, wines from an award-winning cellar, the breath-taking coastal setting, *and* inspired works of art by local artists. Occasionally, the Inn highlights the works of a single artist, in a series of solo exhibitions titled *A Taste of Art*.

The Gallery even extends outdoors, where the art welcomes and intrigues… it frames the parking lot, hangs on the wide front porch, guards the pathways throughout the gardens and lush grounds.

Proprietors Frederique and Sinclair Philip have also decorated each of the guest rooms individually, with utilitarian art of custom-crafted furnishings, fixtures and amenities. The guests of Sooke Harbour House relish this organic approach of incorporating art into every aspect of living. Some have even donated works from their own collections, to be placed in the rooms in which they have stayed. Frederique and Sinclair accept these works with appreciation, and they become part of the Sooke Harbour House's Permanent Collection.

Our Family Project

SOOKE HARBOUR HOUSE BEGAN as a small house on the ocean with a restaurant and five bed and breakfast rooms. The quaint, white, seaside retreat was built in 1929 by Mr. Kohout, a Czechoslovak immigrant. From its conception, Sooke Harbour House functioned as both a home and an inn.

Its setting is magical: primeval forest carpeting the rolling Sooke Hills, mist clinging to the treetops or lying like a scarf along the water, ocean tides rolling in and receding. Once you see it, you fall in love. I know we did, and our guests do too.

Sooke Harbour House, the way it was, 1929

Sooke Harbour House has been our family project since 1979. It all happened like a fairy tale. I met Sinclair Philip in Nice in 1967, only a month after he had arrived in France from Canada. He was, at the time, a young student on his first trip abroad to explore Europe and perfect his French. I think his initial idea was to keep travelling, eventually on to Africa. Instead, he stayed 10 years in France, studying political science and international economics. He earned his PhD, and I completed my Masters of Economics.

During those years in France, we lived in a small village of 400 people at the end of a valley. Although we lived very frugally, we always had large gatherings of friends over for long meals, prepared with **local ingredients** that we usually gathered from our own large vegetable garden and from nearby farmers. Most of our friends were students and artists.

In 1978, we decided to move to Canada, and chose Toronto, then home to Sinclair's mother, as our first destination. We lived there for a year, Sinclair working as a researcher with the Steelworkers' Union, and I doing my best to adapt to a completely new culture, learn English, and be a mom-at-home to my first two children, Benjamin then 11 years old, and Jasmine who was one and a half.

Both Sinclair and I dreamt of leaving the big city, and our dream soon became a reality. On a business trip to Vancouver, Sinclair took two days off to tour Vancouver Island and found Sooke Harbour House. Much to our surprise, we became the owners of an inn!

Benjamin Philip
Our House in St. Paul de Varces

We imagined running the tranquil little B&B in the holistic manner in which we had lived in France. In our minds, the transition from that very peaceful way of life, to being owners of a small business based on similar **values**, seemed simple and straightforward. Ignorance is bliss!

Rissa Philip
(at age 14)
Bounty of the Sea

The Seal Room

I trusted that if we worked hard, offered **local, seasonal cuisine** and comfortable rooms, artistically decorated, we would be successful. And although it was *not* simple or straightforward, my trust was not betrayed. We were successful in the sense that we had a home, (we lived in the basement of the Inn for 16 years), food nicely prepared by our chefs, a garden and a place to expand, transform and mould our lives to match our dreams and aspirations, as we happily raised our four children.

So we have lived and are living our dream. It is based on a solid philosophy of offering our guests the experience of a coastal hotel on the Pacific Ocean, serving local, regional, seasonal cuisine, growing native plants, decorating our rooms with the work of local artists and furnishing them with cabinets, sinks and beds of local craftsmanship.

This book is my first attempt to illustrate the key facets, values and style of our life at the Sooke Harbour House.

Why Start With Art?

ART IS THE FIRST SUBJECT, my first venture into the world of books, because it ***feels*** like it should be. I look inside myself and around me, and search for the answer as to why I feel art should take primacy.

And I ***see*** that art is life. Nature is an artistic masterpiece, from which all art and all life comes.

And I ***feel*** how art is the expression of our heart, our spirit and our soul.

Art was a predominant part of my childhood; the walls of our family home were always adorned with art, not expensive paintings, but with what we found that was beautiful. My mother filled our home with colour and design using posters, cut-outs from magazines, poems glued on the fridge (this was before fridge magnets) and sculptures made from branches collected on our walks. I did not understand back then that my mother looked at the world through artistic eyes. I realized it later, looking back upon my family life and having memories of our colourful home, the busy walls and the attention paid to details.

Rissa Philip
I love you

I am reminded of years ago when my father, the serious business man, decided to paint a large mural on one of the walls in our home in the south of France. It was a colourful, beautiful mural of sailboats on the Mediterranean Sea. While we consider it commonplace, and even expect to receive random artistic expression, usually drawings, from children or young people, it often comes as a great surprise when an adult produces a painting or drawing or a sculpture. It seems that articulation of our feelings through art is discouraged as we grow older. Perhaps, as we perfect our grammar and language to facilitate verbal expression, we leave behind our artistic impulse, our ability and tools to communicate non-verbally.

Feelings, when expressed through art, are in their purest form. They are not vulnerable to transformation and manipulation, which comes with the subjective interpretation of words.

The connotation of art in today's society is far from my definition of the term. For too many people, art comes in a frame or on a pedestal. People buy art after they have met their many other wants and needs; art is what they can afford when there is money left over. To my mind, that is a narrow vision, and looks only at a fraction of the art that surrounds us everyday, everywhere.

Nishka Philip
Self-portrait

Most people recognize in themselves only a minimal amount of artistic skill. Over the last 24 years at Sooke Harbour House, I have discovered a great amount of hidden talent. Such experience has led me to realize that there is art in all of us, that every one of us has artistic talent. Sadly, this talent is very often suppressed by a fear of criticism or fear of not being good enough, but *who is judging*? Thus, so many talents are never nurtured to fruition.

View of Sooke Harbour House

We also assume that we need to have book knowledge to decide whether a piece of art is good or not. We think we need expertise, appropriate schooling and the right words to be able to judge artistic merit. But the only criterion I use is how I feel about the art; I listen to my heart. If I like an art piece, it is therefore a good one for me. The same principle applies to wines. Some people are shy when choosing a wine, for fear that they will choose the wrong one, a bad one. But, like art, a wine that you like is a good wine! And, if you like how it tastes with a certain food, it is a good food and wine pairing.

Derek Heaton & Renaat Marchand
Ocean Sculpture Fence

Seeing Life through Artistic Eyes

FROM THE MOMENT OUR GUESTS ARRIVE at Sooke Harbour House, they are immersed in art, from the edible gardens to our sculptures, from the cushions to the mosaics and paintings. Visitors sit in our dining room and choose from our menu that changes daily, food that is multi-sensual, utilitarian art. Each plate is prepared individually and carefully by one of our chefs, and when presented at the table, our guests have the chance to not only look at this edible work of art, but to smell it and taste it too.

Rockfish

My motivation for providing this wholesome and artistic experience is to encourage people to see life through artistic eyes. With this ability, which if nurtured, is not hard to develop, one's vision of the world is transformed.

A tree is not merely an obstruction to our view nor just a source of wood and fruit. A tree is deep brown, cylindrical, with splashes of bright green leaves and shiny, round red, green and yellow apples...it is art in nature.

Society, magazines and television insinuate that art is something only affordable to the wealthy, but I believe that art can be found even in the most utilitarian objects. For example, the Municipality requested we add more parking spaces around Sooke Harbour House, and it meant losing trees and two of our herb and flower gardens. So we chose to incorporate a visual buffer... a way of hiding the cars from view. In a collaborative, creative process, artists came up with an artistic "fence", but fence is only its utilitarian definition. Most visitors, guests and even we are more inclined to call it the "ocean sculpture", whose main purpose is to be beautiful and whose ability to hide cars is an added benefit!

Since 1979, our beginning at the Sooke Harbour House, we have continuously showcased the artists of our area. We sought local artists to create the themed décor of our guest rooms and found artisans to create an Emily Carr headboard, a fish mirror for the Ichthyologist's Study, a swimming scallop stained-glass window for the underwater orchard and a garden stained- and fusion-glass shower stall. With the help and contribution of two generations of the Newman family, we have designed a whole room around native art. This is our beautiful, large, Potlach room, where you can feel the quietude and serenity of native culture.

Marn Williams
Kitchen Garden Room Shower Stall

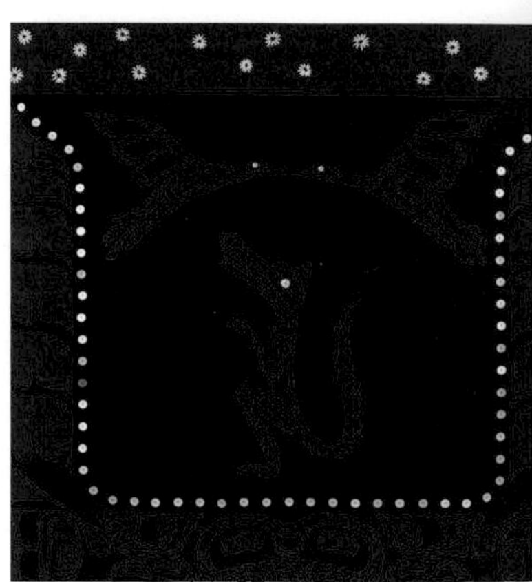

Edith Newman
Philip family button blanket

Reviving Utilitarian Artwork

WE HAVE SO MUCH TO LEARN from the indigenous peoples of our region, whose art existed in all facets of their lives. In their clothing, their bedding, their carpets, and their dishware, every object used in everyday life was a piece of art.

In our modern Western civilization, mass production and the elevation of materialistic values, along with the belief that "time is money", have erased utilitarian artwork from our lives. We do not have the time to embroider our curtains; it is much quicker to buy them. We cannot afford the hours it would take to paint a mural on our wall; it is much more expedient and convenient to purchase printed wall-paper.

However, this pre-fabricated, impersonal lifestyle and design is less conducive to a sense of well-being and contentedness. The lack of creative expression in our modern world leaves people with a sense of discomfort and disconnection. When our cities are designed with a "rationale" of efficiency, and do not introduce art into our lives, through the addition of whimsical details on buildings, or the placement of artfully crafted and comfortable benches among tastefully landscaped gardens or squares, we can perhaps create a city, but we fail to create a community!

Sooke Harbour House thrives because it is an artful celebration of life, of creative expression, and of community. This can be felt in the kitchen full of artist-chefs, in the garden with its creative gardeners and natural processes of creation, in the guest rooms full of artistic craftsmanship, and in the natural surroundings that never cease to inspire.

Sea-view bench,
Sooke Harbour House gardens

Frederique,
on the beach at Whiffen Spit,
below Sooke Harbour House

It is a celebration of people and nature, creating an atmosphere of relaxation, of quiet, and of peace, where we can listen to our hearts, let the barriers down and allow serenity to flow into and among us.

I have always been interested in design and in creating spaces where people want to stay because they are comfortable. I interpret space as a picture puzzle, where all the elements – colour, light, smell, sound, touch – fit together. Then, when the last piece of the puzzle, the person, is placed, the picture is complete.

Human beings need to create and surround themselves with creativity. We are not what we possess; we are what we create. It is for these reasons that this book focuses on art and the artful celebration of life.

Frederique Philip, February 2003

The Recipes: Art on a Plate

I AM PLEASED TO PRESENT YOU with 14 recipes created by our head chef, Edward Tuson. Normally his recipes, (and therefore our daily menus), are inspired by the morning deliveries of fruit, vegetables, meat and fish. However, in this instance, Edward gained the inspiration for each of these recipes from the art included in this book!

Sooke Harbour House Chef Edward Tuson took his training at the Vancouver Vocational Institute in British Columbia, Canada, in 1988. While working in Vancouver, he often spent his spare time snorkelling for abalone in the coastal waters near Sooke, where he met Sinclair Philip, co-owner of Sooke Harbour House. This led to his employment at the Inn in 1990, followed by an intensive five-year apprenticeship.

In the creative cauldron that was and is the Inn's kitchen, he was encouraged to focus on one menu element at a time. Thus he devoted a year or more each to appetizers, vegetables, sauces and pastries. In 1995, Edward left Sooke Harbour House to travel extensively throughout Southeast Asia, where he gained exposure and experience that significantly influenced his culinary craft. In 1999, he returned home and was employed once again by Sooke Harbour House.

The following is an excerpt from an interview that I had with Edward, in which he narrates the process of his inspiration.

Edward: *"...the shading in the pictures themselves inspired me...as I looked at the colours and forms of the pictures, I would think of a dish. For example, I looked at the golden colour of the pears, and I devised the maple roasted pear recipe, in which the fruit takes the same golden hue as in the picture.*

"As I looked at each picture, I wrote down exactly what came to my mind in relation to food, rather than doing it the other way around. It was fun, it was inspirational, and it was easy because I just went with what I thought of; I let my mind freely follow its own creative path.

"So, as you can see, the artwork directly inspired the food, rather than the food inspiring the art."

Frederique: *"You know, it is interesting that when you see something, be it a drawing or a plant or a view, you think food. And sometimes when I am in the kitchen looking at your creations, the sauces and food, I see a room, I see a couch, I see a rug, I see a pillow. It's interesting that one's personal interests bring something different."*

Edward: *"Yes, it is remarkable how the mind works. Your job is your passion, and everything relates back to the thing that you love a lot; for me it is food. I think you see it everywhere, because it is something you are constantly thinking about."*

Frederique: *"Of course! When I see your sauces, which sometimes are incredibly vibrant and colourful, I think of room design and colour schemes."*

Edward: *"It's true that we are inspired by the work of others, in a completely different field, when doing work of our own. To have a dinner based on a picture, a painting... it would definitely be an interesting way of doing a meal..."*

Frederique: *"Well, we could organize that...an art-tasting dinner coupled with a wine-tasting dinner..."*

And so another idea in the artful celebration of life is born at Sooke Harbour House!

Art of Sooke Harbour House

Garnished with Recipes

A note to the reader:

"You'll notice that in each of the artists' biographies on the following pages is a word highlighted in colour. Together they express the values that inform and inspire my family."

Frederique Philip

Bentwood Box Seaweed Broth

Ingredients

1 ounce	dried kombu seaweed (Bull kelp, Laminaria groenlandica)
1	large carrot, peeled and cut into ¼ inch pieces
1	large onion, diced into ½ inch cubes
2 stalks	celery, sliced into ¼ inch pieces
2 stalks	lemon grass, pounded and sliced into ¼ inch pieces
2 tbsp	ginger, coarsely chopped
¼ cup	brown rice or blonde Miso
⅛ cup	Tamari or low sodium soy sauce
6 cups	water
¼ cup	safflower oil

Method

1. Place a four-quart pot over medium heat, and add oil, onions and carrots.
2. Sauté for eight to 10 minutes, stirring occasionally.
3. Add all remaining ingredients and simmer for 75 minutes.
4. Remove from heat, strain, cool and refrigerate until ready to use.

Using a Bentwood Box

1. Place four rocks approximately four inches in diameter and two inches thick in a fireplace until they are red hot.
2. Place the rocks in a Bentwood Box with seafood or shellfish.
3. Quickly add two cups of seaweed broth and place the lid on the box immediately.
4. Steam the fish for five to seven minutes, remove the lid and serve.

Chef's Notes

The broth can be served on its own or used as a soup base.

Mussels, clams or shrimp with their shells work best.

The number of rocks to be used depends on the size of the box.

If done properly, the presentation of the Bentwood Box Broth is spectacular, as the steam will billow out from under the lid.

"This beautiful cooking vessel,
decorated with native drawings of sea animals,
made me think immediately of the sea.

Carey Newman
Bentwood Box
Carved and painted
Red Cedar cooking vessel
12.5"w x 12.75"d x 11"h

Thus, I created a seaweed broth for this box,
in which you can cook a multitude of shellfish."

Edward Tuson

Large Slab Bottle
Hand-built in stoneware clay,
slips and underglazed, high fired
16"w x 10"h

DULCIE DRAPER imbues her artwork with a sense of elegance and humour. She started potting in 1964 at night classes in her local high school in New Zealand. Later she became a member of the Auckland Studio Potters, where a *mentor* encouraged her to hand-build in stoneware clay. Her expertise at her craft has won her many commissions including work for Expo 86 in Vancouver, Petro Canada, the Calgary Exhibition and Stampede and Ducks Unlimited.

Dulcie Draper
250 642-5555
P. O. Box 522
Sooke, B.C. Canada V0S 1N0

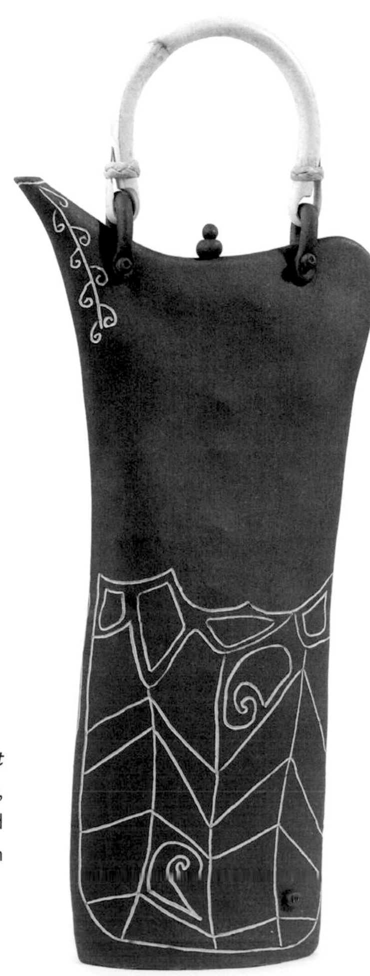

Black Teapot
Hand-built in stoneware clay,
slips and underglazed, high fired
4.5"w x 16.5"h

Large Black Lady
Hand-built in stoneware clay,
slips and underglazed, high fired
6"w x 17"h

Small Black Lady
Hand-built in stoneware clay,
slips and underglazed, high fired
4.5"w x 14"h

Percheron
Oil on canvas
48"w x 60"h

WILL JULSING *creates* strong, brooding works, often with a somewhat eerie quality. He achieves his look with a blend of oil paint and gold; this blend has become somewhat of a trademark as well as the attenuated figures he loves to portray. Born in Groningen, Holland during the German occupation, Will studied art there and in Utrecht. After his art training, he worked commercially for a time. Then in 1966, he was one of 20 painters chosen to represent Holland in an exhibition that toured various European countries. The next year, he made his home in Canada and has exhibited widely here and in the U.S.

Will Julsing
250 748-9905
McLay Road
Duncan, B.C. Canada V9L 6S1

Departure
Oil/gold on canvas
36"w x 36"h

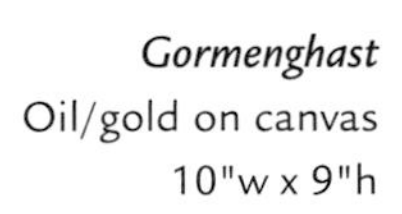

Gormenghast
Oil/gold on canvas
10"w x 9"h

Emerging
Salmon bone, bird bone,
feathers and fabric
21"h

LINDA DANIELSON has worked in the dining room of Sooke Harbour House since 1980, where she is much ***nourished*** by the creative environment. She has also long been involved in textile arts but only lately discovered that her true passion is making art doll figures. Her studio resembles an archeological dig comprised of fabrics, beads, paints, bones, shells, stones, dried foliage and all kinds of wonderful thrift store finds. Using Celtic studies, shamanism and folklore as inspiration, each piece is needle-sculpted, lightly painted and masked. Her work has been included in many local exhibitions and can be found in private collections in Great Britain, Australia, the U.S. and Canada.

Please see page 101 for another image by Linda Danielson, inspiration for the recipe Mussel and Caramelized Onion Tart.

Linda Danielson
250 642-4323
6579 Throup Road
Sooke, B.C. Canada V0S 1N0

Spring
Fabric, feathers
and found objects
21"h

Raven Dancer
Leather, clay, fabric
and findings
22"h
(SOLD)

Dungeness Crab

In Sweet Cicely Broth

Ingredients

1	cooked Dungeness crab, 1.5–2 lbs, with the meat and shells separated
1	large carrot, peeled and cut into ¼ inch slices
1	large onion, coarsely chopped
2 stalks	celery, cut into ¼ inch slices
4 cloves	garlic, thinly sliced
2 tbsp	ginger, coarsely chopped
3 stalks	lemongrass, pounded, and sliced into ¼ inch pieces
½ cup	butter
½ cup	white wine
⅛ cup	sweet cicely, finely chopped
2 cups	Chanterelle mushrooms, sliced into ¼ inch pieces

Method

1. Put the butter in a four-quart pot and melt over medium high heat.
2. Add the onions, the carrot, the celery and the garlic.
3. Sauté the vegetables eight to 10 minutes, stirring constantly.
4. Add all remaining ingredients but the crabmeat, the mushrooms and the sweet cicely.
5. Simmer on low for 90 minutes and strain through a fine mesh strainer.
6. Pour the broth into a two-quart pot.
7. Add the mushrooms, the crabmeat and the sweet cicely; let simmer for two to three minutes and serve.

Chef's Notes

This broth can be served with pasta, mixed vegetables or shellfish.

Sweet cicely can be replaced with fennel, tarragon or basil.

"The crab ~ I thought of the crab
swimming in the ocean
along the bottom of the sea,

Nancy Powell
Black Cat Forge
Crab
Hot forged steel
9"w x 2"h

so I found it fitting

that the crab was made into a broth..."

Edward Tuson

Bull Kelp Basket
Basketry
5"w x 7"d x 7"h

LORI MESSER has no formal art education, but was a fabric weaver before she learned basket weaving from many excellent Pacific Northwest artists, including some Haida elders. She works exclusively in natural materials: bark, roots, willow, vines, kelp, rushes, sedges and grasses. Part of her training included learning how and when to harvest these materials, and how to prepare them. Lori finds working with natural materials very challenging, as there is little uniformity in the material. A part-time artist and full-time Community School Coordinator, Lori finds her weaving to be a "spiral dance", very centering and calming, that keeps her *sane* in a hectic world.

Lori Messer
250 642-4327
RR#4, 7025 Deerlepe Road
Sooke, B.C. Canada V0S 1N0

Rush Hat
Basketry
13"w x 6.5"h

Cedar Clam Basket
Basketry
6w" x 9d" x 11h"

Riverbank Hideout
Fish: Rocky Mountain Juniper, abalone
Base: deer antler
Left front trout 11.6"
Right front trout 10.6"
Rear trout 13.2"

DENNIS DEMARCHI is a wildlife biologist by training, and a ***self-taught*** carver, who uses his knowledge of his subjects' anatomy and habits, gained in his formal education, to inform his art. Initially, his main interest was in wooden decoys but that expanded to include detailed water birds and trout. There are several of his gulls on display in Sooke Harbour House, including one flying over the large dining room table. (The Philips have a strong emotional attachment to seagull images, as Sinclair's mother loved gulls and the ocean.) Dennis works primarily with local woods: Western Red Cedar, Rocky Mountain Juniper and Big-leaf Maple. He was born and raised in the interior of British Columbia.

Dennis Demarchi
250 382-7372
2816 Shoreline Drive
Victoria, B.C. Canada V9B 1M6

Liberta
Western Red Cedar,
glass and oil paint
22"w x 8.5"d x 3.9"h

Glaucous-Winged Gull, Standing
Western Red Cedar, steel,
glass and oil paint
Base: Western Hemlock
16.1"w x 5.5"d x 13.6"h (without base)

Flowers in the Garden
Oil on panel
16"w x 20"h

SUSAN ELKINS, impressionist painter, uses colour to express the arrangements and harmonies of her subjects. Whether painting a landscape or still life, she realizes it is vital to ***truthfully*** portray natural light. With vibrant, subtle or more somber hues, she faithfully captures bright sun-filled gardens, foggy damp lush fields, or a quiet lane on a hazy afternoon. She has participated in group and solo exhibitions across Canada and her work is found in both corporate and private collections. She received the education that most influenced her at The Cape School of Art in Provincetown, Massachusetts.

Susan Elkins
Susan Elkins Studio
403 762-3728
Box 714
Banff, Alberta, Canada T1L 1A7

Overlooking the Strait
Oil on panel
16"w x 12"h

Indoor Still Life with Conch Shell
Oil on panel
14"w x 11"h

Fisherman's Room Sink
Ceramic
17"w x 6"d

ALICE MCLEAN discovered pottery after studying and working in many different fields, including medical technology and film animation. Her work includes a wide variety of functional and non-functional sculptural objects. Custom-made sinks are a specialty; many have found a home in the rooms of Sooke Harbour House and in beautiful private homes as well. Alice also crafts decorative indoor and outdoor fountains. The *magical* process of potting...creating artful, functional objects out of mud...has completely captivated her. And she is most grateful to her late husband, Barry, for providing equipment, building kilns and registering her in classes.

Alice McLean
250 642-3522
962 Gillespie Road
East Sooke, B.C. Canada V0S 1N0

Kitchen Garden Room Sink
Ceramic
17"w x 6"d

Fish Bowl Sink
Ceramic
17"w x 6"d

Sole Wrapped Lingcod with Chive Crust

Ingredients

6	sole filets, 6 inches long minimum
6	three ounce lingcod pieces, preferably from the head end
¼ cup	chives, coarsely chopped
¼ cup	unsalted butter
¼ cup	breadcrumbs
½ tsp	salt
½ tsp	finely ground pepper
1 clove	garlic, minced
3	leek greens, 8–10" long, blanched

Method

1. Preheat oven to 400 degrees Fahrenheit.
2. Cut leek greens in half lengthwise for tying.
3. Season sole filet with salt and pepper, wrap around lingcod and tie bundle with the leek strip. Place fish in the fridge.
4. Place chives, butter, breadcrumbs, garlic, salt and pepper in food processor for four to five minutes, or until smooth. Remove from food processor and place in a small bowl.
5. Remove sole lingcod roll and place one and a half tablespoons of chive crust on top of each fish roll. Place rolls on a well-oiled baking sheet and bake for 10–12 minutes or until the crust starts to brown on top.

Chef's Notes

Sole varieties that can be used are Lemon, Dover, Petrale and Rock sole.

This dish is delicious served with tomato or pesto sauce or with a Rose Petal, Johnny Jump Up Vinaigrette. As an accompaniment, try **Buckwheat Noodle Salad** or **Roasted Sweet Peppers**. (See pages 62 and 90.)

"When I saw this sole and lingcod picture,
I imagined the fish swimming together,
frolicking in the ocean,

Dinah Giffin
Ling Cod, Sole
Acrylic
20"w x 30"h

so I created a recipe
of sole-wrapped lingcod!"

Edward Tuson

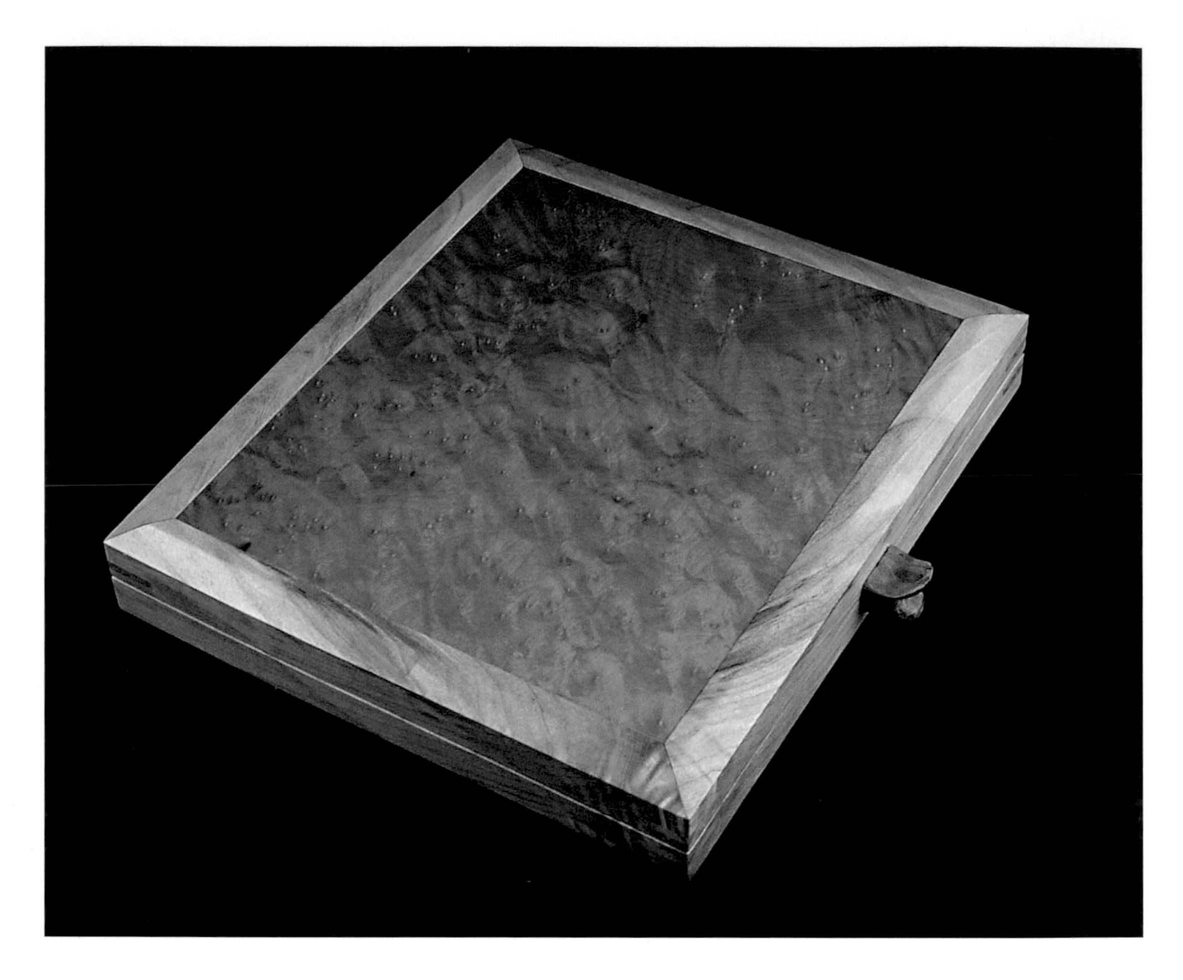

Silver Spoon box
Madrone burl and Big Leaf Maple
7"w x 8"d x 1.5"h

Robert Martin recently set aside his job as a *Philosophy* professor to turn his life-long passion of working in wood, into a career. An artist who takes inspiration from natural forms, he believes that a wood creation should live as long and as gracefully as a tree. In fact, he is now working on a 15 foot tall "tree bed" for the Raven's Nest room at Sooke Harbour House. Robert's custom furniture and wood art has been displayed at the Sooke Fine Arts Show and in an exhibition at the University of Victoria's Maltwood Museum.

Robert Martin
Custom Furniture and Wood Art
250 642-3051
8485 West Coast Road
Sooke, B.C. Canada V0S 1N0

ABOVE

Carved Rose Vine Table
White Oak
36"w x 14"d x 24"h

ABOVE

Carved Rose Vine Table
Detail

Weary Bones
Walnut and Red Oak
12"w x 12"d x 24"h

KERRY GORTAN grew up in a small community on Vancouver Island, where he learned to work with wood from his father. This skill was to remain a constant in his life. As a teen, Kerry made handcrafted furniture, and when he was older, he worked as a carpenter.

Gradually, Kerry began to explore other aspects of wood, through carving and sculpting. He enjoys making West Coast art such as masks, totem poles and stone sculptures. Upon request, Kerry also creates *family* portrait totem poles and portrait masks. His work is sold at Sooke Harbour House and he has exhibited at recent Sooke Fine Arts shows.

Kerry Gortan
250 642-1855 or 250 514-5133
6574 Tideview
Sooke, B.C. Canada V0S 1N0

Family Tree
Fir
18" in circumference x 84"h

West Coast Warrior
Spalted Maple burl
8"w x 12"h

Swimming Grays
Whale bone and
soapstone sculpture
7 lbs, 12"w x 12"h

Sparkling Golden Sea
Traditional Japanese painting (*Nihonga*)
16"w x 22"h

KIMIKO specializes in the medium of *Nihonga*, traditional Japanese painting. Instead of oils, the *Nihonga* artist uses powdered, *organic* mineral pigments that are bound to Japanese parchment with a natural glue. Kimiko prefers floral subjects but has also done extensive work in landscape and figures. She has completed a 12-painting series depicting the flowers of each month in Japan and is now at work on a similar series for the flowers of British Columbia. Before moving to Canada in 1997, Kimiko was awarded first place from among approximately 250 entrants at the Tokyo Kodaira Art Show in 1996.

Kimiko
250 655-3469
11187 Hedgerow Drive
North Saanich, B.C Canada V8L 5S3

Crimson Forest
Traditional Japanese painting (*Nihonga*)
20.5"w x 17.5"h

Joseph's Coat
Traditional Japanese painting (*Nihonga*)
9"w x 10"h

Seared Scallop Salad

with Pickled Daikon Radish

Ingredients

12	swimming scallops
1	leek green, blanched
	vegetable oil, salt and pepper
¼ cup	Daikon radish, julienned
¼ cup	sea lettuce
¼ cup	seaweed (Laminaria)
2 tbsp	pumpkin seeds, toasted
1 tbsp	shallots, minced
½ tsp	garlic, minced
2 tbsp	pumpkin seed oil
	Arugula flowers
	Mustard flowers
	sea salt

Pickle Solution

¼ cup	pear cider vinegar
¼ cup	white sugar
1 tsp	sea salt
1 tsp	ginger, minced
½ cup	water

Method

1. Combine vinegar, sugar, salt, ginger and water in a saucepan. Bring to a boil, take off heat and allow to cool.
2. Julienne Daikon radish into thin strips approximately two inches long. Pour cooled pickle solution over Daikon radish and let sit at least one hour.
3. Rinse seaweed thoroughly and slice into thin strips, (same as Daikon).
4. In a bowl, mix pumpkin seed oil, salt, shallots, garlic, drained Daikon and seaweed into a salad mixture.
5. Cut leek greens in half lengthwise for tying.
6. Tie scallops in bunches of three with the blanched leek.
7. Sear scallops in a hot pan for approximately two minutes each side.
8. Toss pumpkin seeds and flowers into salad mixture.
9. Assemble salad mixture and seared scallops on plates.

Chef's Notes

These scallops, cooled or warm, make a great addition to a marinated salad.

The scallops are attractive and delicious when baked in the half shell and served as an hors d'oeuvre.

The scallops could also be steamed and served with the Sole Lingcod roll for a more elaborate seafood meal or used as a soup garnish in any variety of tomato, cream or broth-based soups.

Note: all of the recipes, with the exception of this one, were inspired by the art. In this case, the recipe came first and inspired an original painting.

Gillian Ley

Hot Pot series

Gouache/watercolour/ink

9"w x 12"h

Fantastical Birds
Clay sculpture, clay, glazes, metal
Smallest 4"h to largest 12"h

GLENYS MARSHALL-INMAN cannot remember a time in her life that *art* was not important to her; it was a major focus in both her family life and early schooling. In her work, Glenys explores the use of clay in many different forms: functional pottery, sculptural pieces and painting on paper clay. She credits wonderful teachers from the 'clay world', and encouragement from her husband and family with enabling her to live a life blessed creatively, everyday. Among her experience, Glenys counts many solo and group exhibitions in Canada, Greece and New Zealand. In 2001, Glenys founded the Orveas Bay ~ Otter Point Gallery and Studio and is now concentrating on her own studio work.

Glenys Marshall-Inman
250 642-5555
4565 Otter Point Road
Sooke, B.C. Canada V0S 1N0

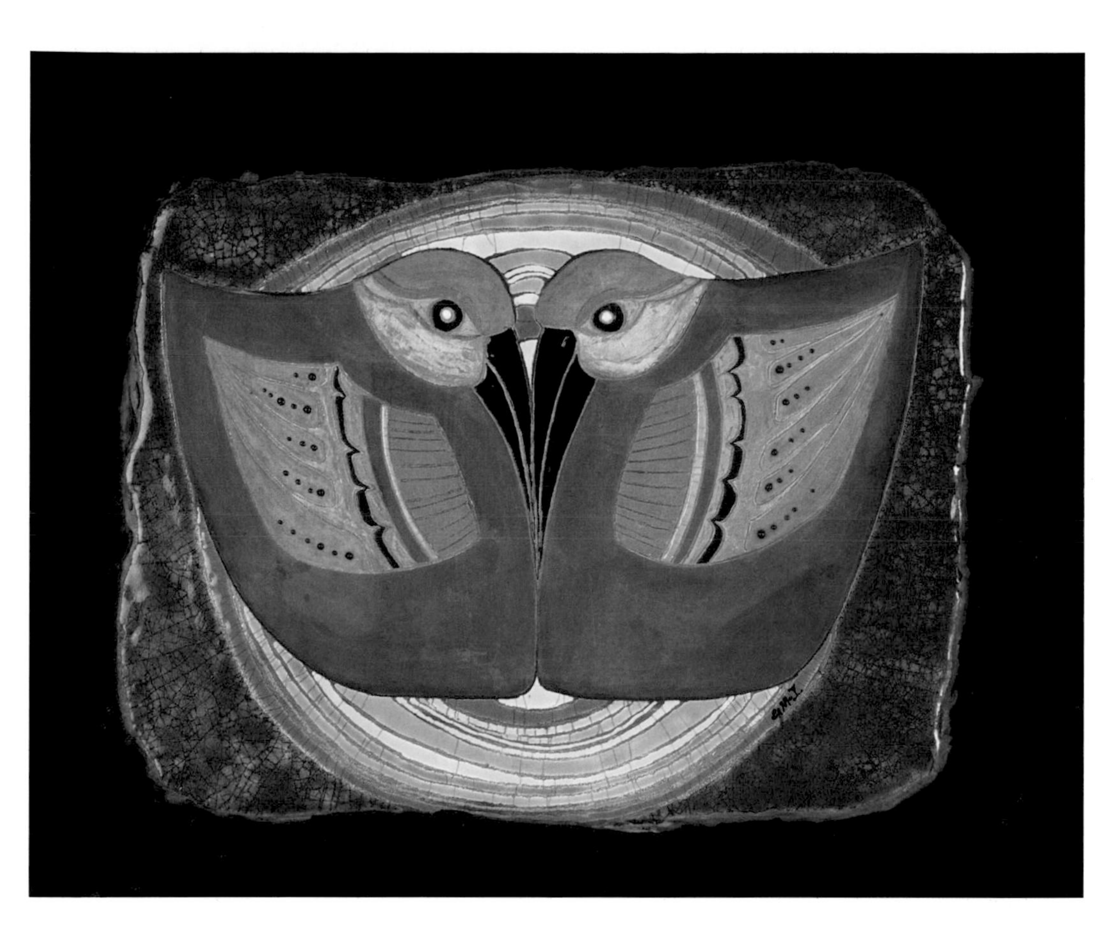

Sublime Together
Paper clay painting, paper, clay,
clay slips burnished and glazes
24"w x 20"h framed

Fantastical Bird
Paper clay painting,
paper, clay, glazes
14"w x 14"h framed

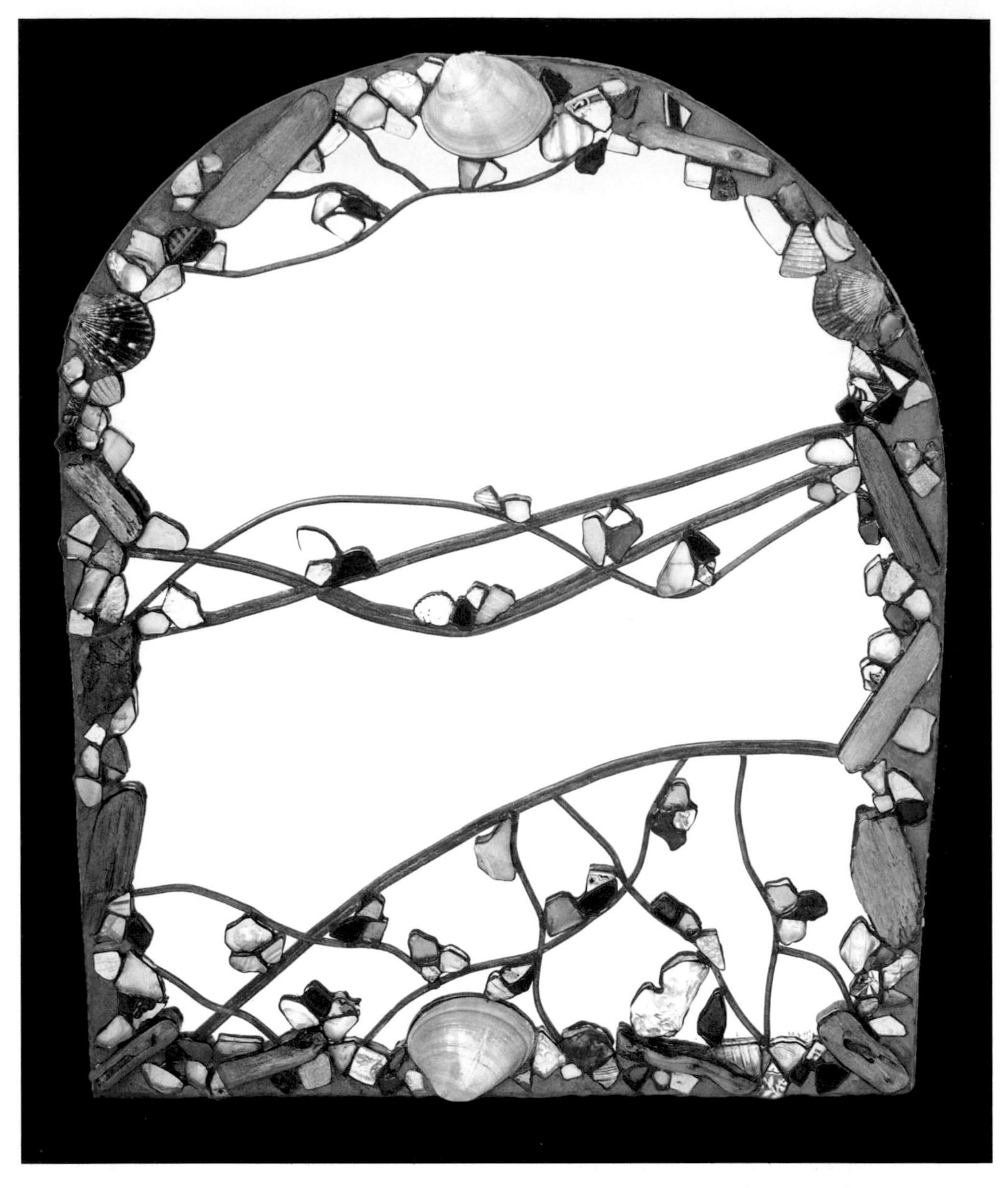

Seawaves Mirror
Found beach glass, worked in the
Tiffany style of stained glass assembly
24"w x 30"h

NORRA MIROSEVIC collects beach glass, some of which is over 100 years old, for her sparkling, colourful works of utilitarian art. Originally from shipwrecks and canneries, the glass and ceramic shards are tumbled by the powerful sea to become the raw material for her votives, lamps, jewelry, mirrors and other decorative works. Using wire wrapping and copper foiling techniques, she creates original designs that are a blend of ***history***, beauty and artistic skill. She also accepts commissions. Self-taught, Norra is continuously developing creative and unusual ways to work with the treasures from the sea.

Norra Mirosevic
Beach Glass Creations
250 477-2255
2521 Sinclair Road
Victoria, B.C. Canada V8N 1B3

Boudoir Lamp
Beach glass, in Tiffany style
5"w x 12"h

Votive grouping
Beach glass, in Tiffany style
9"w x 6"h

Equinox sunflower
Iron work
3'w x 3'h

SANDY SYDNAM was first introduced to blacksmithing as a child in Toronto, when visiting Ontario's Black Creek Pioneer Village. A very small, delicate child, she was content to sit on the smith's plank floor and watch for hours. When she announced she wanted to be a blacksmith when she grew up, her father laughed and said that was not something girls did. Now her father is very ***proud*** of his daughter, who uses traditional forging methods and many different types of steel in her work. Also a practitioner of Judo since age five, Sandy feels Judo has made an invaluable contribution to her life and her art.

Sandy Sydnam
The Bellowing Blacksmith
250 642-7225
RR#6, 5931 Leda Road
East Sooke, B.C. Canada V0S 1N0

Backwater Tranquility
Iron work
11"h x 7"w

Spawned Out
Iron work
29"w x 17"h

Tuscany
Art photography
16"w x 12"h

SIMON DES ROCHERS is a Canadian photographer who spent many years in England and France. He combines surreal, digitally manipulated photography with a trans-Atlantic sense of ***humour*** to create intriguing and thought-provoking images. Masterful invention of time, space and mood is a compelling element of his work. His captivating images have been published in numerous Canadian and international magazines.

Simon Des Rochers
250 382-3637
1818 Government Street, Studio 2003
Victoria. B.C. Canada V8T 4N5

Enlightenment
Art photography
20"w x 26"h

Cured Hecate Strait Halibut

Ingredients

8 ounces	fresh halibut (the thinner fish is, the faster it will cure)
¼ cup	brown rice Miso or blonde Miso
½ cup	water
⅛ cup	Tamari or Low Sodium Soya Sauce
1 tbsp	ginger, minced
1 tsp	garlic, minced
1 tbsp	rosemary, finely chopped
2 tbsp	honey

Method

1. In a medium-sized bowl, mix all ingredients except the halibut.
2. Pour this marinade into a non-corrosive loaf tin; add halibut.
3. Cover and refrigerate for three days. Turn the halibut daily.
4. Remove the halibut from the marinade and pat it dry.
   The halibut should be firm when pinched between your fingers.

Chef's Notes

This halibut can be cooked any number of ways.
It is juicy and tender when barbequed, can be sliced thin and served on greens, or cubed and added to potato salad.

Also, try slicing the halibut approximately half inch thick, grilling it and placing it in a soup, or perhaps using the meat as ravioli or perogy filling.

"Then I came across Craig's halibut,
and I looked closely at the halibut,

Craig Benson
Pacific Halibut
Soapstone sculpture
260 lbs, 40"w x 27"d x 7"h

and saw amber and green tones,
which made me think of Miso and Soya sauce..."

Edward Tuson

La Famille
Family of four seals, Brazilian soapstone
17"w x 9"d x 8"h

WALLY HEAD feels he cannot explain his newfound ***talent*** to create lasting artworks in stone; he considers it a gift. And it was only when major surgery forced Wally into early retirement from the pulp and paper industry that he began to discover his talent. It was his interest in lapidary, wood carving, prospecting and rock-hounding that drew him to stone carving. Eventually he settled on soapstone as his medium of choice. This material, with its spiritual feel, has allowed the artistic gift to flow through his hands.

Wally has also created concrete cast artworks, which he hand-finishes and produces in limited editions. Some of these creations can be found in the gardens of Sooke Harbour House.

Wally Head
250 746-6127
6350 Woodgrove Place
Duncan, B.C. Canada V9L 5R4

Let's Do Lunch
Eagle on Cod, Brazilian soapstone
33 lbs, 13"w x 12"d x 8"h

Swan
Pink soapstone
11"w x 10"d x 5.5"h

Sunset on the North Shore
Limited edition Giclée print
40"w x 22"h

PAUL GRIGNON was always drawing and painting as a child, and began working in oils at the age of 13. Later, a year at Toronto's New School of Art fully awakened his "artist's *soul*". In 1973, he moved to Gabriola Island in B.C. where he worked as a tree planter and at construction, as well as doing commercial and fine art. An injury eventually steered him into making a full-time living from his art. He began in 1982, when he spent a year building a diorama exhibit for a local museum. Paul then pursued a wide variety of artistic projects, such as painting murals and theatre sets, while simultaneously exhibiting and selling his fine art in galleries across Canada. Since then, recognition of his work has grown steadily. He has recently gained international exposure at New York City's Art Expo, the Fall Fair in Birmingham, England and through a one-man show in Carmel, California.

Paul Grignon
Moonfire Studio
250 247-8350 or 8012; toll free: 1 866 839-8273
2525 Coho Drive
Gabriola, B.C. Canada V0R 1X7

Washed in Gold
Limited edition Giclée print
36"w x 14"h

Divine Afternoon
Limited edition Giclée print
30"w x 12"h

NANCY POWELL started blacksmithing at the Sooke Regional Museum in 1991. Enchanted by the noise, smell, dirt and sparks, she forged a career for herself as an artist. Using a combination of modern and old tools, she creates her art *freehand*, without jigs or forms.

Nancy hammers out a wide variety of original pieces, from kitchen and bathroom fixtures to exquisite mermaids. Since 1999, she has worked her forge in "the most beautiful blacksmith's shop in the world", located at Sooke Harbour House. Custom orders are a big part of Nancy's work, which can be found from Seattle to New York, and in Australia and Japan.

Before becoming a blacksmith, Nancy worked as a cook at Sooke Harbour House.

Please see pages 25 and 121 for other images by Nancy Powell, inspiration for the recipes Dungeness Crab in Sweet Cicely Broth *and* Honey Roasted Chicken Stuffed with Garlic and Herbs.

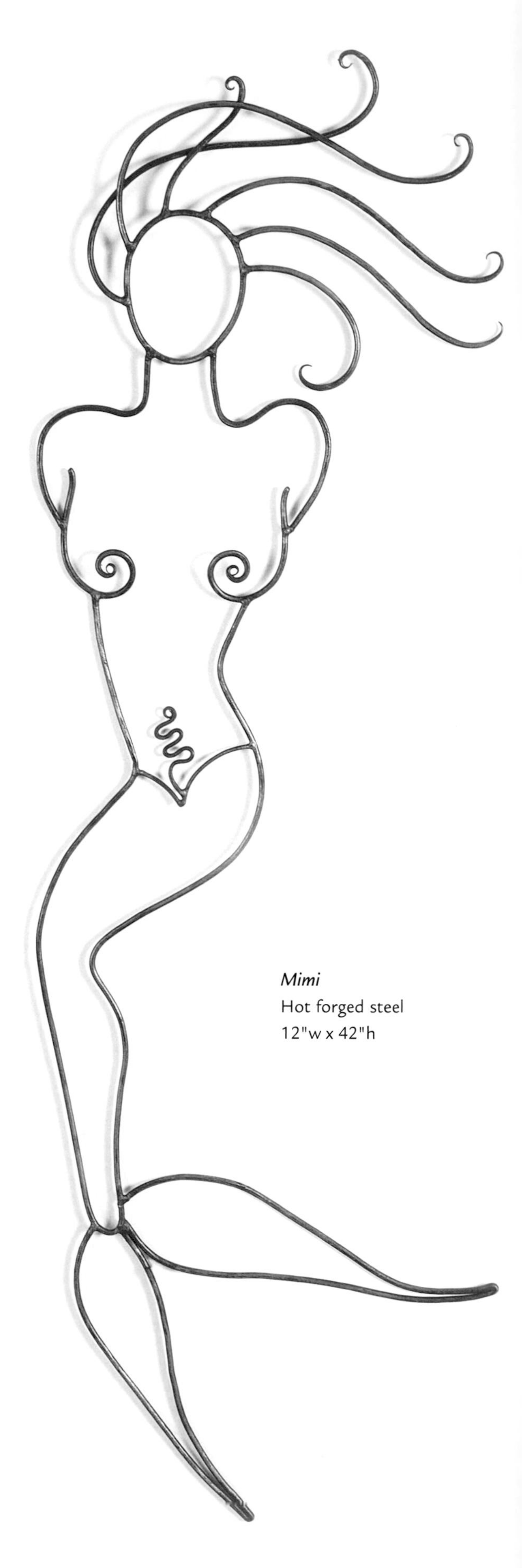

Mimi
Hot forged steel
12"w x 42"h

Nancy Powell
Black Cat Forge
250 478-2942
1020 Liberty Drive
Victoria, B.C. Canada V9C 4H9

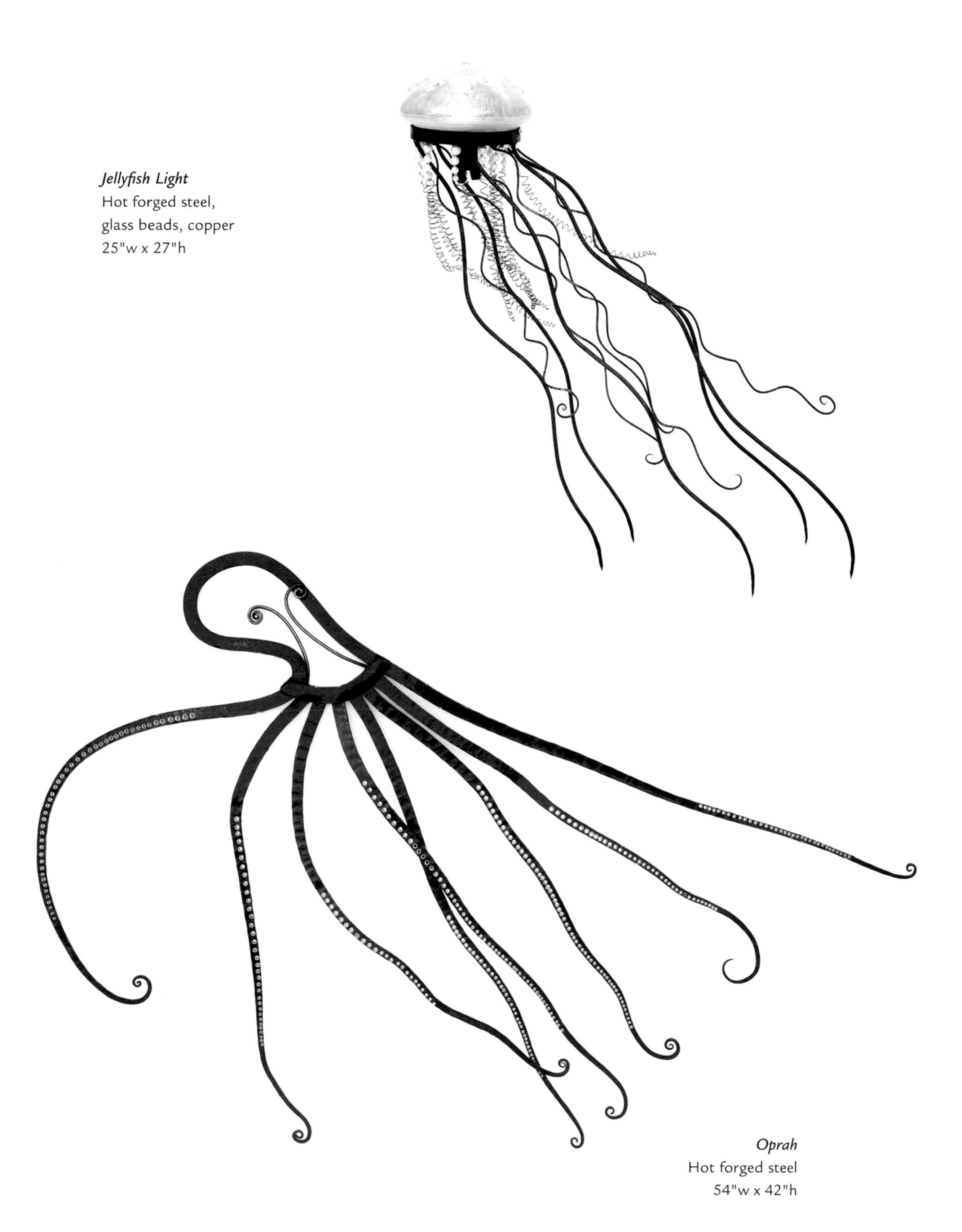

Jellyfish Light
Hot forged steel,
glass beads, copper
25"w x 27"h

Oprah
Hot forged steel
54"w x 42"h

3 Heads
Basketry
12"w x 14"h

ANNE BOQUIST was working at Sooke Harbour House in the early 1980s, when she began weaving highly ***original*** baskets of unusual materials. One of her best customers in those early years was Frederique Philip, who used them as bread-baskets in the dining room. When guests asked if they could buy the baskets right off the tables, Frederique allowed them, and suggested that Anne and her mentor, Kathy Johannesson, sell their wares in the Inn's Gift Shop. The two artists then entered the first Sooke Fine Arts Show and jointly won the Juror's Choice Award. Anne's work is now found in private collections in Canada, the United States and Europe, including the Bronfmann Foundation Collection.

Anne Boquist
250 642-3798
3183 Robinson Road
Sooke, B.C. Canada V0S 1N0

God's Eyes
Basketry
14"w x 14"h

Halibut Basket
Basketry
12"w x 22"h

Coriander Crusted Albacore Tuna

with Spicy Buckwheat Noodle Salad

Crusted Albacore Tuna

Ingredients

12–14 oz.	Albacore tuna loin, chilled
2 tbsp	ground coriander seed
1 tbsp	coarsely ground pepper
1 tbsp	salt
¼ cup	safflower oil

Method

1. Place coriander, salt and pepper in a small bowl and mix well.
2. Slice the chilled tuna in half.
3. Rub the spice mixture onto the tuna, being sure to spread it evenly all sides.
4. Heat oil in a large frying pan on high heat, until the oil reaches smoking point.
5. Carefully add the tuna and sear it for two minutes on each side.
6. Remove the tuna from the pan, and refrigerate it for a minimum of 30 minutes.

Spicy Buckwheat Noodle Salad

Ingredients

2 cups	cooked buckwheat noodles
⅓ cup	grated carrot
⅓ cup	grated celery
⅓ cup	grated turnip or Daikon
¼ cup	finely chopped red onion
2	cloves of garlic, minced
1 tbsp	minced ginger
⅛ cup	finely chopped green onion
2 tbsp	Soya Sauce
2 tbsp	finely chopped Jalepeño pepper
¼ cup	mayonnaise
¼ cup	sour cream

Method

1. Place all ingredients except the noodles in a medium-sized bowl and mix well.
2. Add the noodles and mix until they are well-coated.
3. Cover and refrigerate for one hour.
4. Remove the noodle salad from the fridge and fill a three-quarters measuring cup with the noodle salad.
5. Pack the noodles down with a measuring cup.
6. Place a fork in the middle of the salad and twist to wrap the noodles around the fork and remove them from the measuring cup.
7. Place the noodles in the centre of a plate.
8. Slice the chilled tuna half inch thick and place it on top of the noodle vegetable salad.

Chef's Notes

The seared tuna is also delectable when served on steamed rice, couscous or salad greens.

Try using the tuna cubed, as a soup garnish, or mixed with pickled beets, walnuts and Feta cheese.

The noodle salad also makes a fine accompaniment for **Cured Hecate Strait Halibut**. (See page 52.)

Dinah Giffin
Tuna
Acrylic
22"w x 10"h

"The tuna is interesting because when I saw it,
my mind produced an image of it
swimming through a forest of bull kelp,
and the bull kelp made me think
of a forest of noodles."

Edward Tuson

Naramata Benchland
Acrylic on canvas
40"w x 30"h

CHRISTINE REIMER strives to "create energy with paint and canvas that can be experienced by the viewer". She does so with vibrant colours dynamically interwoven with vigorous brushwork. Working with her favourite medium, acrylics, she depicts West Coast landscapes, Okanagan vineyards and orchards, *exotic* gardens and whimsical paintings of people and creatures. Represented by six art galleries across Canada, her artwork is in corporate and private collections throughout North America. Frederique and Sinclair Philip have also been steady patrons of Christine's work for many years. She has participated in major exhibitions across western Canada, as well as international juried exhibits.

Christine Reimer, B.F.A, DIP.ED.
250 592-3525
1951 Woodley Road
Victoria, B.C. Canada V8P 1K4

Galiano Island Lagoon
Acrylic on canvas
46"w x 32"h

At Newcastle Island
Acrylic on canvas
30"w x 24"h

Foraging Grizzly
Acrylic
40"w x 30"h

DINAH GIFFIN paints to capture precious moments and convey her love of nature. She particularly loves to paint the elusive creatures of the sea: fish, octopus, otters. Delighting in the abundant beauty of the West Coast, Dinah feels she is *blessed* with opportunity and subjects.

She was born in Toronto, Ontario and all through elementary, junior and high school her entire focus was art, art, art. Dinah graduated with Honours from the University of Victoria with a Bachelor of Fine Arts degree. Following graduation, she represented the Fine Art Department for The Helen Pitt award in Vancouver. Dinah has exhibited in both Sooke and Victoria.

Please see pages 35 and 63 for other images by Dinah Giffin, inspiration for the recipes Sole-Wrapped Lingcod with Chive Crust *and* Coriander Crusted Albacore Tuna with Spicy Buckwheat Noodle Salad.

Dinah Giffin
250 744-2875
121 Conard Street
Victoria, B.C. Canada V8Z 5G3

Siesta
Acrylic
26"w x 29"h

MARN WILLIAMS AND SUSAN ISAAC are both glass artists and co-owners of Shards Glass Studio, which opened in 1998. Here they create fused glassware, cast glass art pieces and leaded or foiled glass architectural panels that often include fused and kiln cast, or sculpted glass features. They draw inspiration from their forested, rural neighbourhood and the near-by ocean.

Susan and Marn were first introduced to glass fusing in 1997, and since then have been taught the skill by some of the best glass artists in Canada and the U.S. The fusing and casting technique allows for new dimensions of texture and depth not usually seen in traditional windows. Marn's fused glassware is sought as far afield as Japan and Australia. He also did all of the stained glass windows in the first Sooke Harbour House expansion, in 1986.

Please see page 81 for another image by Susan Isaac, inspiration for the recipe Lavender Crème Brulée.

Marn Williams and Susan Isaac
Shards Glass Studio
250 642-7424
3809 Otter Point Road
Sooke, B.C. Canada V0S 1N0

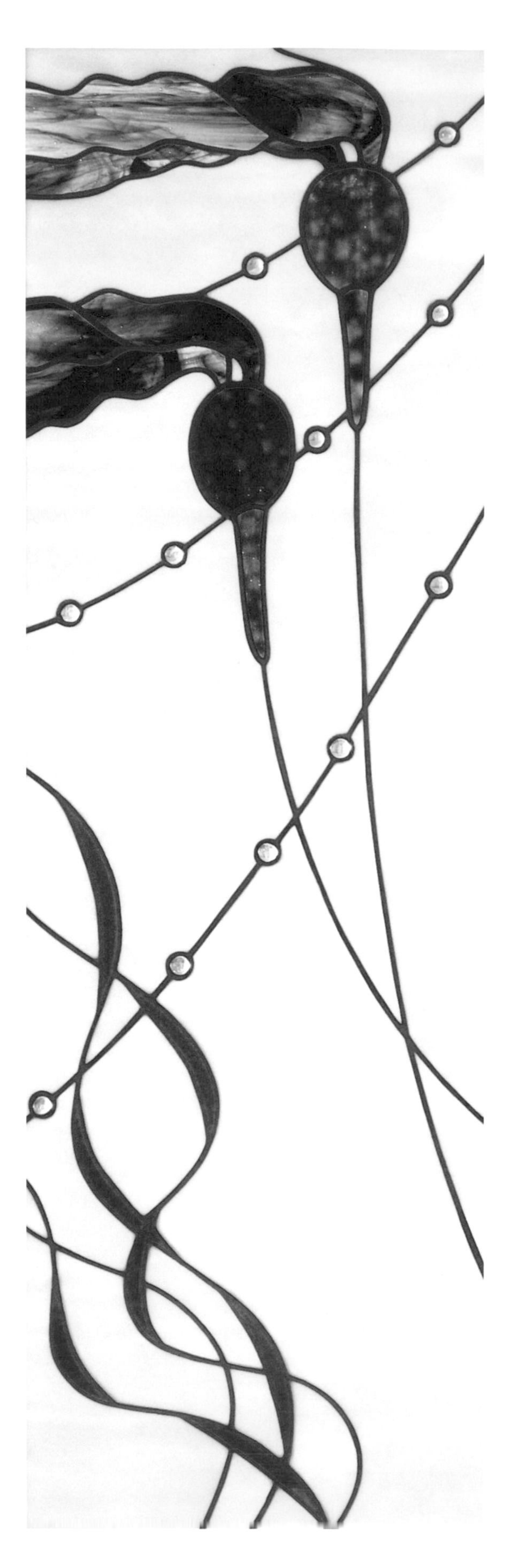

Seaweed Window
Bull kelp and sea grass in glass, foiled
16"w x 42"h

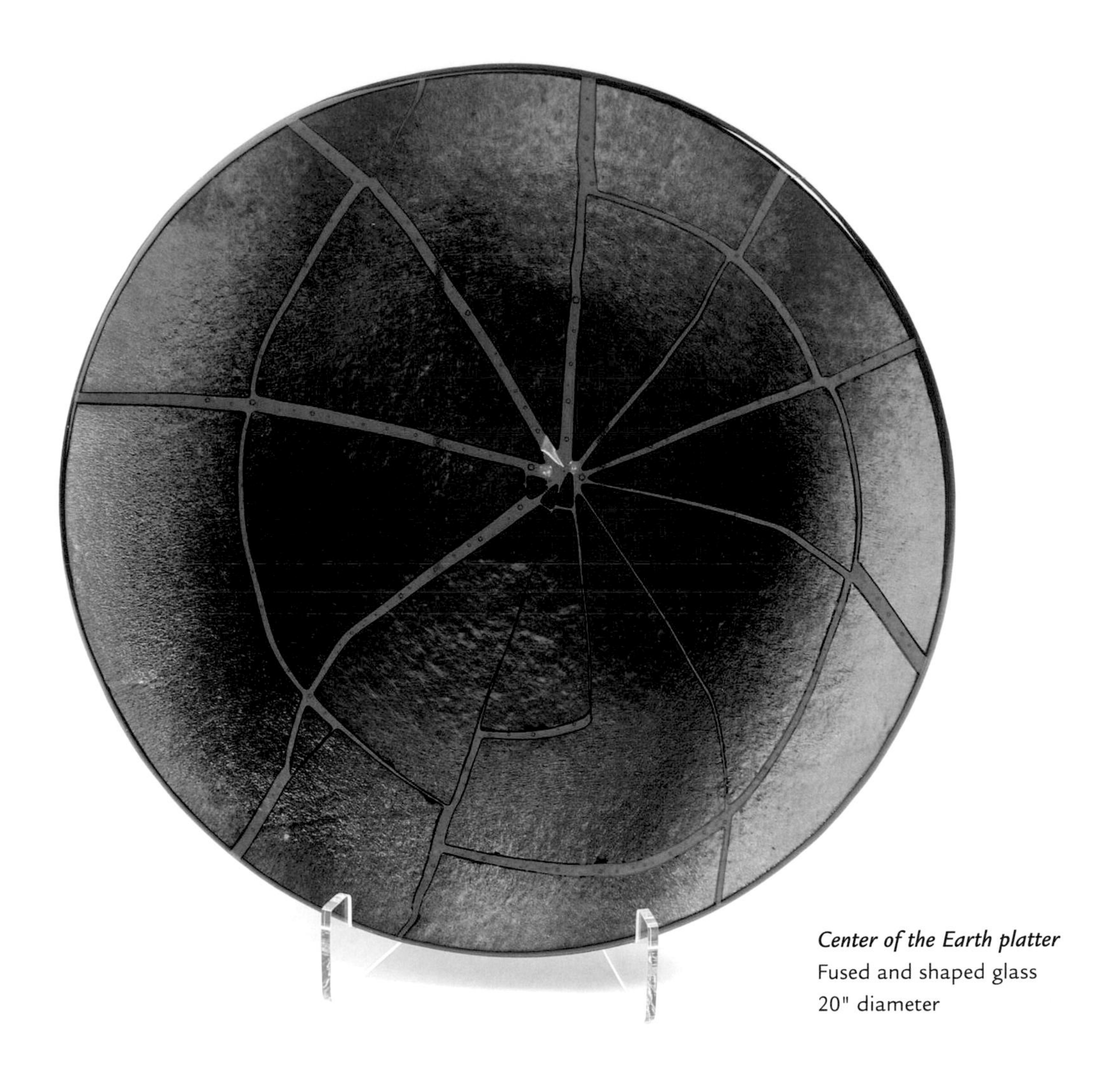

Center of the Earth platter
Fused and shaped glass
20" diameter

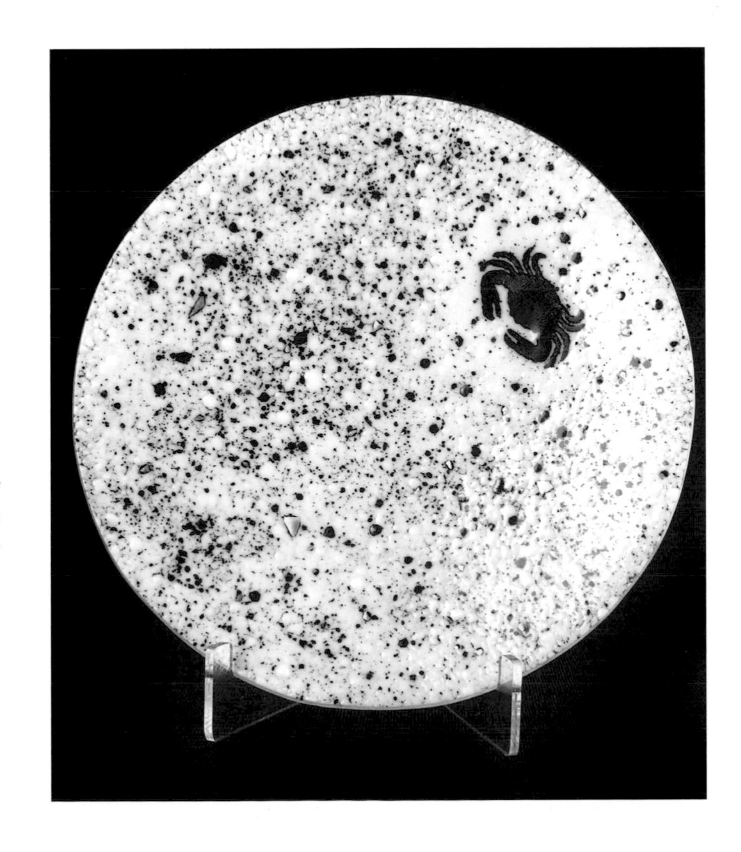

Blue Rock Crab #8 platter
Fused and shaped glass
17" diameter

Wooden Bowls
Yellow Cedar Burl
Upper: 14"w x 6"h
Lower: 18"w x 8.5"h

AIVARS LOGINS has a unique ability to reveal the inner beauty within the grain, textures and irregularities of wood. All of the wood in Aivars' works is native to the Sooke area; much of it is considered logging waste and destined to be burned. He rescues these leavings and in his oceanside studio, creates beautiful bowls, boxes, platters, mirrors, kitchen-ware, burled furniture and carvings of the highest quality. All pieces are finished with a non-toxic beeswax or 100% pure unrefined tung oil, to retain the natural beauty and patina of the wood. His artistry and ***passion*** for wood have made his work known and collected around the world. Aivars is currently carving a loveseat from a seven foot diameter Western Red Cedar burl which is 800 years old.

Aivars Logins
250 642-4603
8520 West Coast Road
Sooke, B.C. Canada V0S 1N0

Red Cedar Burl Bowl
Carved from a 300-year-old tree
15"h, 21" diameter

Yellow Cedar Burl Bowl
Carved from an 800-year-old tree
9.5"h, 24" diameter

Roasted Pumpkin Soup

with Apple Pear Compote

Roasted Pumpkin Soup

Ingredients

1	pumpkin, 2-3 lbs
1	large onion, chopped coarse
1	large carrot, peeled, sliced into ¼ inch pieces
4	cloves garlic, sliced thin
¼ cup	butter
¼ cup	safflower oil
2 tbsp	finely chopped fresh sage
6 cups	chicken or vegetable stock
pinch	salt
pinch	pepper

Method

1. Preheat the oven to 350 degrees Fahrenheit.
2. Cut the pumpkin in half and remove the seeds with a large spoon.
3. Place the pumpkin cut-side down on an oiled baking sheet and bake for 40 to 50 minutes, or until the flesh of the pumpkin is very soft.
4. Remove from oven and let cool for 20 minutes in the fridge.
5. Once cool, scrape the flesh from the skin and place it in a bowl. Discard the skin.
6. Put the butter and the oil in a four-quart pot over medium heat.
7. Add the onions and the carrots; sauté for eight to 10 minutes.
8. Add garlic and cook for another two minutes, stirring constantly.
9. Add the stock and roasted pumpkin.
10. Simmer for 35 to 40 minutes.
11. Remove from heat and let cool for 15 minutes.
12. Puree on high speed in a blender in small batches, until all of the soup is blended and smooth.
13. Reheat the soup with the fresh sage and serve with apple and pear compote.

Chef's Notes

Substitute squash for the pumpkin or replace the honey with maple syrup and the result is equally as delicious

Apple Pear Compote

Ingredients

2	Braeburn, Granny Smith or Royal Gala apples
2	Bosc, Bartlett or Anjou pears
1 cup	apple juice
¼ cup	white wine vinegar
¼ cup	honey
1 tsp	Mustard seed
2 tbsp	unsalted butter
¼ cup	safflower oil
2 tbsp	minced ginger

Method

1. Peel and dice the apples and pears into half-inch cubes.
2. In large sauté pan, place the oil and butter over medium-high heat.
3. Once the butter has melted, add the pear and apple cubes. Sauté for eight to 10 minutes, or until the fruit starts to soften.
4. Add all remaining ingredients and reduce, (i.e. simmer on low), until the liquid is barely visible.
5. Remove from heat and place one heaping tablespoon in the middle of each serving of roasted pumpkin soup.

Chef's Notes

Pears should be firm and not over-ripe.

Whipped cream makes a nice garnish for this dish.

When reheating the compote, add a little butter and apple juice.

d.a. farley

Fruit on Holiday with Squash
Acrylic on panel
28"w x 24"h

Jug of Roses
Acrylic on panel
24"w x 32"h

d.a.farley is originally from Quebec, where he grew up around an art ***tradition*** that was somehow folksy, severe, and accomplished, all at the same time. When he started creating art, (after moving to British Columbia), he instinctively drew upon those earlier images and themes to "wake up the muse". The West Coast influence resulted in works less pressured by tradition and therefore far more relaxed. Deane feels there is an openness on the West Coast that frees up old ideas. Currently his work is handled exclusively by Sooke Harbour House; he has also shown at the Sooke Fine Arts Show and at the Maltwood Gallery, University of Victoria.

Please see page 73 for another image by d.a. farley, inspiration for the recipe Roasted Pumpkin Soup with Apple Pear Compote.

d.a. farley
250 381-6020
915 Empress Avenue
Victoria, B.C. Canada V8T 1N8

Fallen Apple
Acrylic on panel
20"w x 24"h

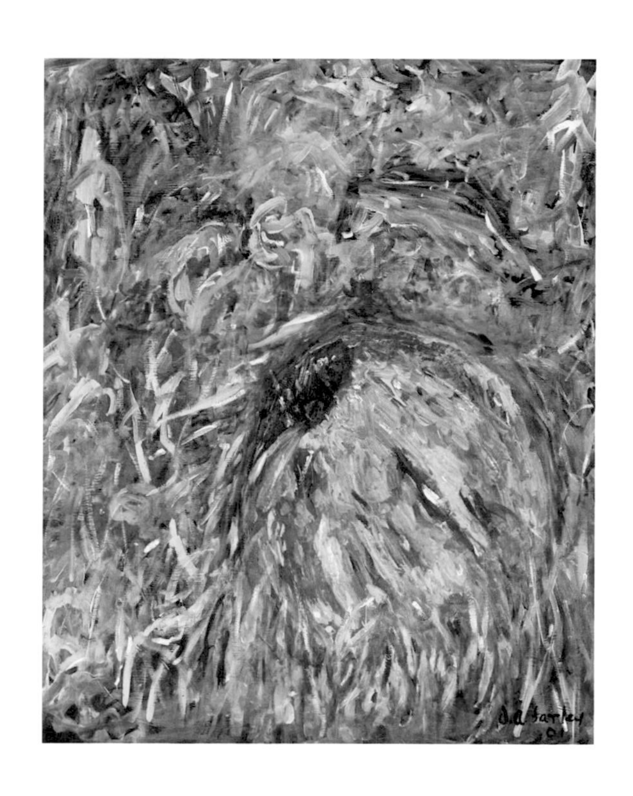

Poppies on a Blue Table
Acrylic on panel
24"w x 32"h

SHEILA BEECH, felt maker extraordinaire, lives and works in Sooke's first district courthouse and jail, which she has converted to be her ***home***, bed and breakfast and studio shop. Rich colours and innovative designs are the hallmark of her wearable art, GnomeKnocker slippers, and designs for interiors. Her work can be found in collections, and closets, worldwide. Sheila has also made felt for New York designer Donna Karan and for the New York Metropolitan Opera. Her work has been selected for many juried art shows, most recently the Sooke Fine Arts Show.

Sheila Beech
250 642-7176
2050 Drennan Street
Sooke, B.C. Canada V0S 1N0

Hand-felted Vest
Hand-dyed wool and mohair
handmade felt
20"w x 30"h

Hand-felted Coat
Hand-dyed wool
and mohair
22"w x 39"h

GnomeKnockers Slippers
Handmade felt
Various sizes

Malahat
Acrylic on canvas
16"w x 20"h

DENNIS SHIELDS finds colour a magical source for his art. His "*experience* of conscious exploration and renewal within the world of colour" affirms for him the oft-quoted lines of J.W. Goethe that, "colours are the results of the deeds and sufferings of light." Prior to entering the School of Painting at the Rudolph Steiner Institute in Switzerland in 1973, he toured the famed art museums of Great Britain, Holland and Italy. Born in North Vancouver, Dennis eventually returned to the West Coast, where he takes his inspiration from his natural surroundings. In addition to Sooke Harbour House, his work is displayed in the Art Gallery of Greater Victoria's Art Rental and Sales.

Dennis Shields
250 370-2462
8 - 1091 Joan Crescent
Victoria, B.C. Canada V8S 3L3

Naramata
Acrylic on canvas
20"w x 16"h

Swiftsure
Acrylic on canvas
20"w x 24"h

Lavender Crème Brulée

Ingredients

1½ cups	32-35% whipping cream
1 cup	homogenized milk, 3.25% MF
¼ cup	sugar
¼ cup	honey
2	whole eggs
2	egg yolks
1 tbsp	dried lavender flowers

6 ramekins, 4-ounce or small bowls

Method

1. Preheat oven to 275 degrees Fahrenheit.
2. Place the cream, milk and lavender in a two-quart pot and warm over medium high heat.
3. Stir frequently while the milk is heating.
4. Place the eggs, the yolks, the sugar and honey in a medium-sized bowl and whisk until pale yellow.
5. Once the cream mixture has come to a boil, remove from heat and let rest for five minutes.
6. Slowly add the hot cream mixture to the egg and yolk mixture. Mix constantly with a rubber spatula, not a whisk. (You do not want to incorporate air while mixing.)
7. Once the mixtures are well blended, strain through a fine strainer to remove the lavender.
8. While the mixture is still warm, pour into the ramekins to one-quarter inch from the top.
9. Place the ramekins in a 9 x 11 cake pan, fill the cake pan three-quarters full with water and then place in the oven.
10. Cook for 40 minutes. The crème brulée is done if the centre barely jiggles when you move the ramekins.
11. Once done, remove from the oven and let cool in the water to room temperature.
12. Remove the ramekins from the water and refrigerate for one hour.
13. Pull the ramekins from the fridge and sprinkle each with a half teaspoon of sugar.
14. Place ramekins on a baking sheet, with the oven rack on the second level from the top.
15. Caramelize by broiling for two to three minutes.

Chef's Notes

Serve the Lavender Crème Brulée with sorbet or cookies.

Instead of caramelized sugar on top, use fruit purée, warm chocolate or caramel sauce.

This crème brulée also goes extremely well with the **Maple Syrup Roasted Pears** on page 110.

Peaches and lavender are also an excellent combination.

Vinegar can be infused with lavender.

Lavender goes very well with tomatoes and can be incorporated into salsa.

Instead of bread crumbs, a rub of lavender flowers can be used to crust fish.

Lavender makes bread even more aromatic and savory sauces more flavourful.

Susan Isaac
Lavender Vase
Fused and shaped glass
8"h

"When I saw the lavender vase,
I immediately thought of
something sweet."

Edward Tuson

Riverside
Giclée print
30"w x 36"h

KEITH HISCOCK'S paintings are invitations to ***contemplation***. His compelling acrylics draw you in, after they've drawn you across the room. Born in Victoria, British Columbia, Keith found his niche in art early in life and worked for some time as an abstract artist, then as a film animation cell painter. When he discovered representational realism, Keith developed his own unique style, a dramatic combination of exquisite attention to detail and powerful scope. He is self-taught and works in acrylic on canvas and panel, applying many layers of transparent and opaque paint. The result is a painting with an inner glow. Keith is one of Vancouver Island's most prolific publishers of limited edition prints; of the 50 he has published, he has sold an estimated 12,000 copies and many editions are sold out.

Keith Hiscock
250 727-6414
4155 Oakridge Crescent
Victoria, B.C. Canada V8Z 4X8

Shells
Limited edition reproduction
31"w x 15.5"h

The Sentinel
Limited edition reproduction
16"w x 15"h

Harbour Seal Head
Original bronze
Limited edition of 35
5"w x 6"d x 3"h

CRAIG BENSON celebrates and honours the creatures on this planet with his work, particularly those of the Pacific Northwest. He was born in Vancouver and moved to Victoria, British Columbia in 1987. Carving began as a hobby for Craig, while he was pursuing an education in environmental studies. His career in wildlife management and habitat protection kept him close to his artistic subjects, and helped develop his appreciation of life's ***diversity***. After several years, his life-long interest in art and nature called him to change careers. At first he sought seasonal employment, to support his art, and then became a full-time carver in 1990. Each of his works is carved from a single piece of wood or stone. The raw piece and its life force suggest a creature within; Craig carves to "release" the creature. His works have been featured in many prestigious exhibitions over the years and he was one of the first artists to have works included in the private collection of Sooke Harbour House. (Despite persistent offers, Frederique will not part with one of his earlier works, a carved seal that resides in the dining room at Sooke Harbour House.)

Please see page 53 for another image by Craig Benson, inspiration for the recipe Cured Hecate Strait Halibut.

Craig Benson
250 656-3617
23 McKenzie Crescent
Sidney (Piers Island), B.C. Canada V8L 5Y7

White Seal Pair
Soapstone sculpture
30 lbs, 17"w x 8"d x 9"h

Mother and Baby Seal
Soapstone sculpture
345 lbs, 42"w x 18"d x 18"h

Island Trail
Hand-cast paper made from B.C. botanicals, embedded with dried, wild B.C. plant life
21"w x 16"h

Daniel Tracy creates handmade Earth Art using native and naturalized British Columbian plants embedded in hand-cast paper. His love of nature and the Canadian West Coast, where he was born, compelled him to study ***indigenous*** botanicals. While making his living as a tree planter, Dan began working in his unique art form. He then developed it further at his residence by the sea. The paper in his works is totally hand-cast from local plants and he uses natural dyes whenever possible. With his Earth Art, Dan transplants the wild beauty of the coast, indoors.

Dan Tracy
604 943-4744
1132 Walalee Drive
Delta, B.C. Canada V4M 2M1

Summer Stroll
Hand-cast paper made from B.C. botanicals,
embedded with dried wild B.C. plant life
22"w x 17"h

River's Edge
Hand-cast paper made from B.C. botanicals,
embedded with dried wild B.C. plant life
25"w x 17"h

Ron Robb
Two Birds bowl
Hand formed, burnished and raku fired
7"w x 7"h

JAN LOVEWELL and RON ROBB formed Rare Earth Pottery in 1995 and have worked in ***partnership*** ever since. For several years previously, Jan made collages and nature photographs, including macro photography of flowers. Now she has returned to pottery, where she continues to explore symbol, form and texture by creating hand-formed, burnished and raku-fired works of art. Ron has exhibited in various media, including painting, photography, seriography and ceramics. Regarding his pottery primarily as an aesthetic and symbolic art form, he has made both classical and experimental forms, freehand. Jan and Ron are currently represented by several galleries in British Columbia, including Sooke Harbour House.

Jan Lovewell and Ron Robb
Rare Earth Pottery
604 483-4806
C. 41, RR#2, Malaspina Road
Powell River, B.C. Canada V8A 4Z3

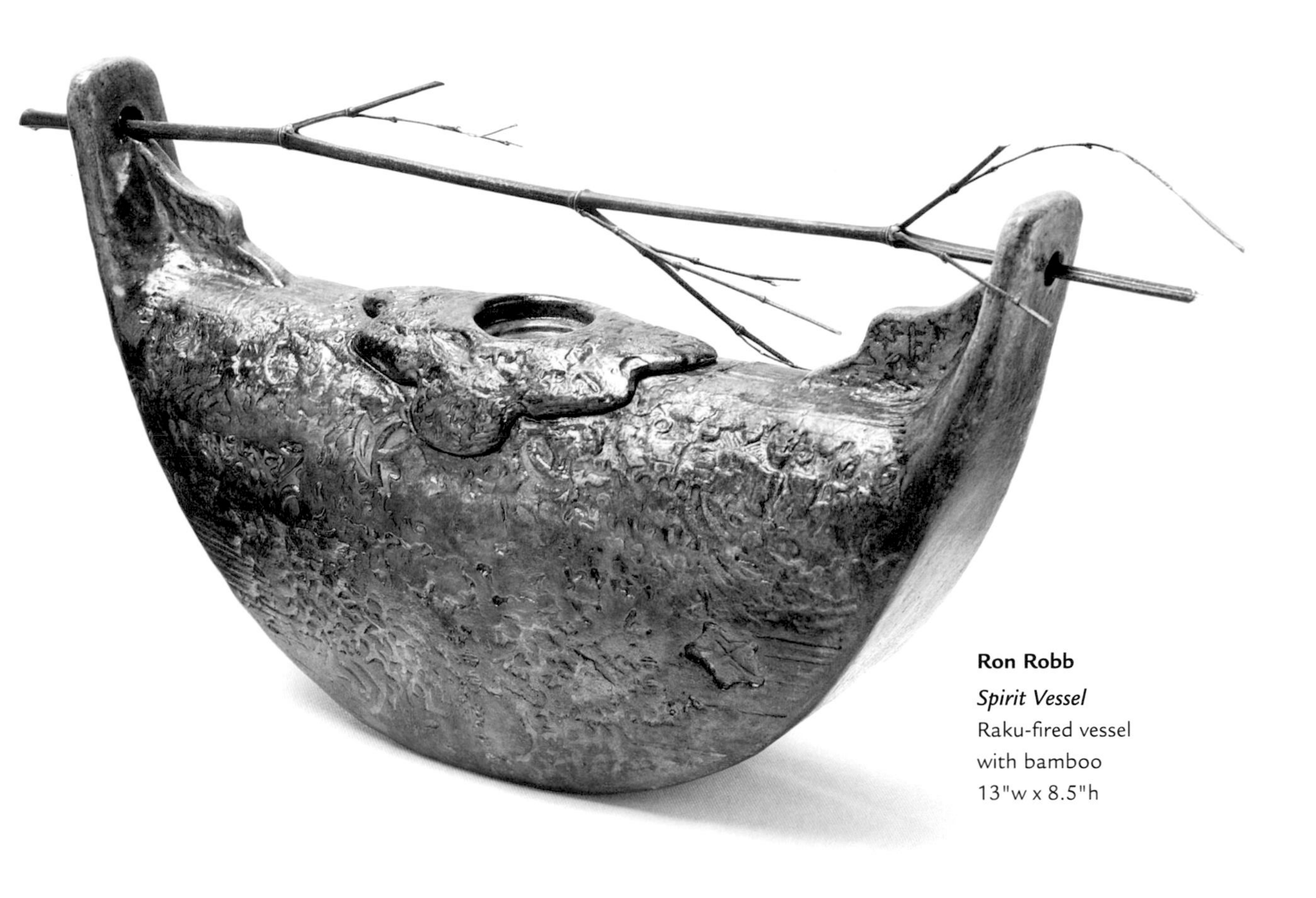

Ron Robb
Spirit Vessel
Raku-fired vessel
with bamboo
13"w x 8.5"h

Jan Lovewell
The Lovers
Hand formed, burnished
and raku fired jar
4"w x 5"h

Roasted Sweet Pepper

Stuffed with Wild Rice and Dried Cranberries

Ingredients

6	red peppers, small to medium
1 cup	wild rice, cooked (¼ cup uncooked)
1 cup	celery, sliced ¼ inch thick
½ cup	dried cranberries
¾ cup	apple juice
½ cup	onion, diced in ¼ inch cubes
2 cloves	garlic, minced
⅓ cup	safflower oil

Method

1. Preheat the oven to 350 degrees Fahrenheit.
2. Bring apple juice to a boil, pour over the cranberries and cover.
3. Soak the cranberries in the apple juice for 30 minutes, then remove cranberries.
4. In a small frying pan, sauté the onions and celery in the oil over medium heat, until the onions are translucent and the celery is softened.
5. Add the garlic and cook for another two minutes.
6. Add the apple juice, and reduce, (simmer on low), until almost no apple juice is visible in the pan.
7. Remove the reduction from the pan and place it in a medium-sized bowl.
8. Add the wild rice, soaked cranberries and oregano to the celery and onion and stir well.
9. Season with the salt and pepper.
10. Cut one-quarter inch off the bottom of the red peppers and one-half inch off the top. Remove the core and the seeds.
11. Brush each pepper with the safflower oil and stuff them with the wild rice filling.
12. Replace the top of the pepper and place the stuffed and capped peppers on an oiled baking sheet.
13. Bake for 30–35 minutes.
14. The peppers are done when they begin to soften or the skin on the pepper just starts split.

Chef's Notes

These stuffed peppers are a great accompaniment for almost any main course. They will be a hit with **Roasted Chicken** (see page 120) or the **Sole-wrapped Lingcod** (see page 34).

The peppers are great with any tomato-based sauce.

You can also substitute your favourite herb for the oregano.

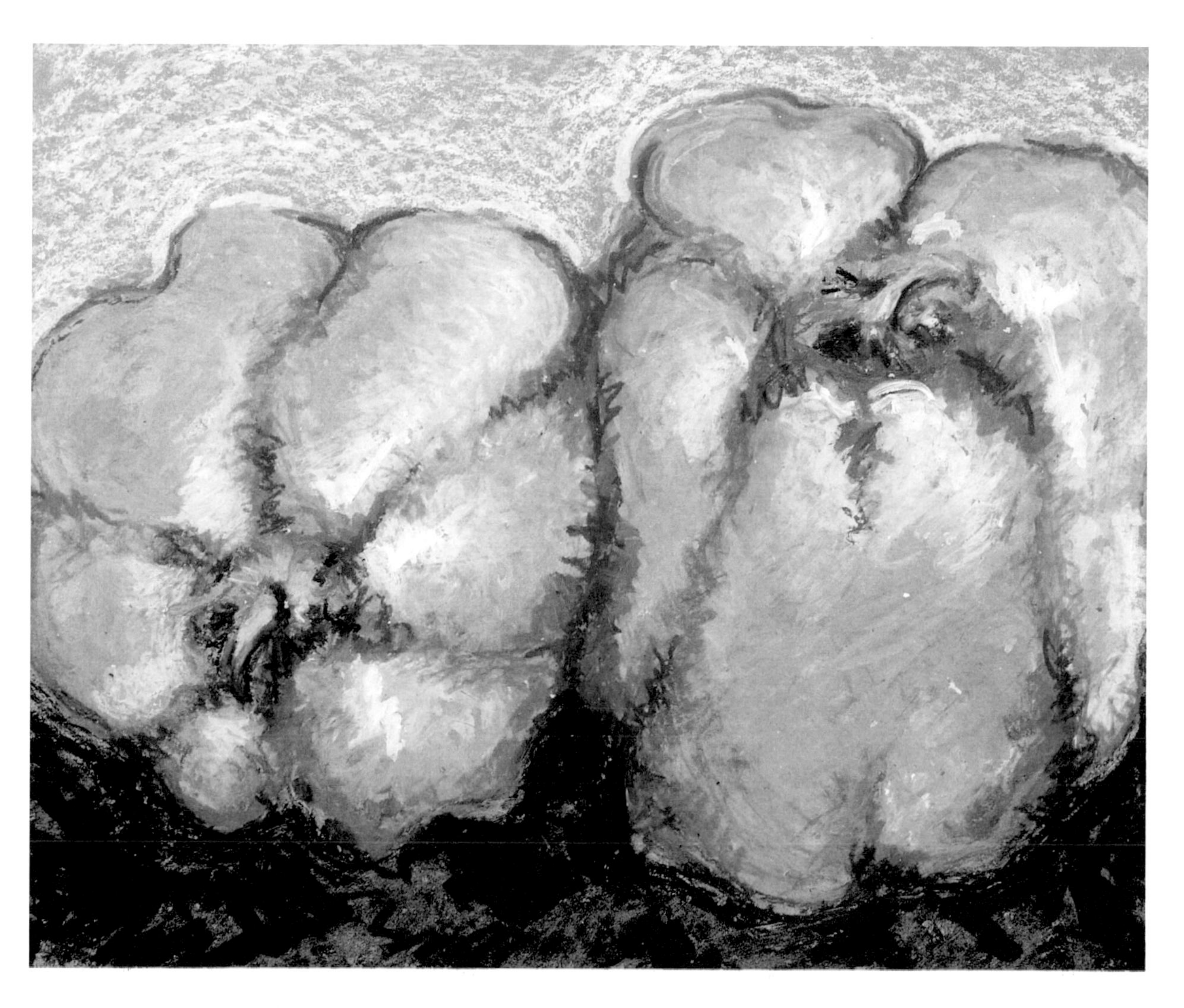

Nishka Philip
Yellow Peppers
Oil pastel drawing
10.5"w x 8.5"h

"When I looked at Nishka's peppers, I thought of roasted peppers almost immediately. There were some darker reds underneath the peppers, which brought to mind cranberries and earth tones, so I thought of wild rice and cranberries, and then of stuffing the roasted peppers."

Edward Tuson

Soul Mates
Oil pastel
15"w x 11"h

RINTJE RAAP always had a creative outlet over his many years of working as a chemist and a teacher. First it was photography, then drawing and finally painting, which added an exciting new dimension to his life. His favourite medium is oil pastel, which he applies on watercolour paper with his fingers. Rintje revels in the vibrant colours and the intimate, tactile connection. The medium also suits his interest in natural, sculpted forms. Compelled to paint, art represents *freedom* to Rintje. In the past two years, he has participated in several group or joint exhibitions in Sooke and Victoria.

Rintje Raap
250 642-0280
414-1061 Fort Street
Victoria, B.C. Canada V8V 5A1

Sunset at French Beach
Oil pastel
22"w x 15"h

Driftwood at Sandcut Beach
Oil pastel
22"w x 15"h

KIM NILSON is a self-taught carver whose work incorporates abstract images with realism. Many intriguing images are portrayed in each piece, whether it is crafted in wood, soapstone, marble or alabaster. The material itself influences his work, so that the carving may evolve from the original concept, invigorating the final presentation with much more vitality. Kim carves with chisel and mallet, preferring the quiet intimacy of these tools to noisy power tools. He has a great respect for ***nature*** and wildlife, which is reflected in his work. Kim has exhibited in both Sooke and Victoria.

Kim Nilson
250 744-2875
121 Conard Street
Victoria, B.C. Canada V8Z 5G3

For a Meadow Landscape
Douglas Fir
18"w x 78"h

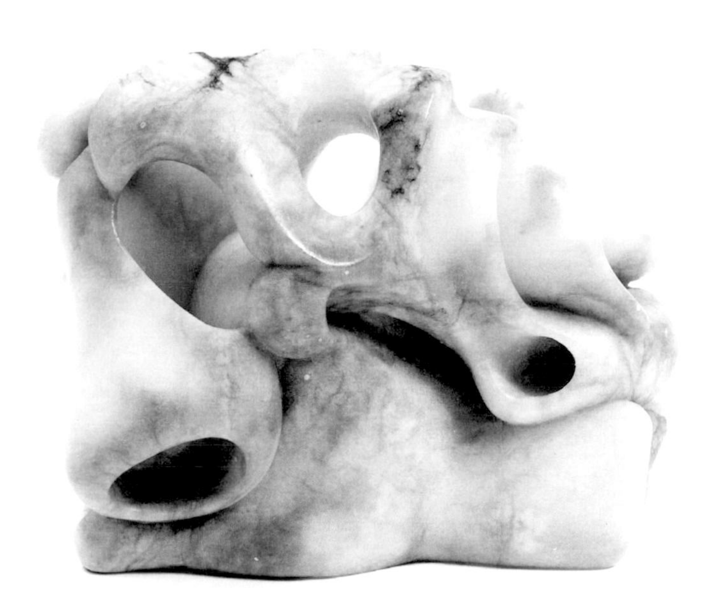

Caprice
Alabaster sculpture
6"w x 6"d x 8"h

Grey Whale: United
Soapstone
15"w x 11"d x 7"h

Salt and Pepper
Intaglio print
9.75"w x 15"h

NISHKA PHILIP is a Visual Arts student at the University of Victoria, who works primarily in printmaking, (intaglio), painting and sculpture. She credits her parents, Sinclair and Frederique Philip of Sooke Harbour House, and their passion for art and natural beauty with leading her to appreciate visual brilliance in all its forms. The themes Nishka explores in her artwork evoke her West Coast surroundings: the trees, the ocean, and because of her unique upbringing at Sooke Harbour House, the food that is a result of such pure, natural ***bounty***.

Please see pages 91 and 131 for other images by Nishka Philip, inspiration for the recipes Herbal Tea Spritzer *and* Roasted Sweet Pepper Stuffed with Wild Rice and Dried Cranberry.

Nishka Philip
250 642-2236
1528 Whiffenspit Road
Sooke, B.C. Canada V0S 1N0

Forest
Acrylic painting
48"w x 60"h

Whiffin Spit from the Garden at Sooke Harbour House
Oil on board
28"w x 22"h

Michel Des Rochers is an accomplished artist who has travelled widely, lived abroad and exhibited extensively. For the past 35 years, he has created paintings in a variety of media: oils, pastels and watercolours. Many of these works have been purchased by private collectors, as well as various municipalities, businesses and museums, such as the Royal Maritime Museum in Greenwich, England. While living in France, Michel took part in many group exhibitions and also enjoyed several successful one-man shows. In 1987, Michel returned to Canada and continued painting, gaining even more extensive ***recognition***.

One of his images, *"The Logger"*, was recently selected by the Canadian Museum of Civilization as a backdrop in its permanent West Coast exhibition. Michel and his wife, Marion, own their own fine art gallery in Sooke.

Michel Des Rochers
250 642-6411 or toll-free 1 800 956-4278
6790 Westcoast Road, Box 507
Sooke, B.C. Canada V0S 1N0

Non Potable
Oil on board
28"w x 36"h

Whiffin Spit
Oil on board
28"w x 22"h

Mussel and Caramelized Onion Tart

Ingredients

1 lb	mussels (preferably Salt Spring Island or Penn Cove)
5	yellow onions, peeled, halved and cut into ¼ inch slices
3 cloves	garlic, minced
1½ cups	coarsely grated Feta cheese
¼ cup	unsalted butter
¼ cup	safflower oil
1 cup	white wine
¼ cup	finely chopped fennel greens
1	basic pie dough, based on two cups of flour

Method

1. Preheat oven to 350 degrees Fahrenheit.
2. Line a 10-inch or 12-inch flan mould with pie dough and blind bake until golden brown. (Blind bake: place parchment paper in the pie shell and fill with beans.)
3. Remove from the oven and cool to room temperature.
4. In a four-quart pot, place the mussels and white wine and cook over high heat.
5. When the mussels all open, pull from the heat, remove the mussels from the pot and place them in the fridge.
6. Once cool, pull the mussels from the their shells. Discard the shells.
7. Do not discard wine and mussel juice. Strain it and refrigerate.
8. Place the oil and butter in the four-quart pot over medium high heat.
9. Once the butter has melted, add the onions. Do not stir for five to seven minutes. Then stir every four to five minutes, until the onions are golden brown.
10. Add the garlic and cook for three more minutes.
11. Add reserved white wine mussel juice and simmer until completely evaporated.
12. Remove the onions from the heat. Leave them in the pot and let cool to room temperature.
13. Add the mussel meat and fennel and stir gently, but well.
14. Place the mussel, onion mixture in the tart shell and cover evenly with Feta cheese.
15. Bake 10 minutes, or until the cheese just starts to brown.
16. Remove from the oven, and let rest for three to four minutes before cutting.

Chef's Notes

Serve this tart with salad greens or baked fish.

Substitute chives or basil for the fennel.

For a stronger flavour, replace the Feta with Blue cheese, Stilton or Cambazola cheese.

Blind baking makes for an even, flat bake; pastry always cooks better when put in the oven cold.

"Linda's doll is carrying a platter of mussels and shellfish, and I thought of her doll walking to the table with a mussel tart..."

Edward Tuson

LEFT

Linda Danielson

Molly Mussel

Shells, dried foliage and fabric

15"h

ABOVE

Linda Danielson

Molly Mussel, detail

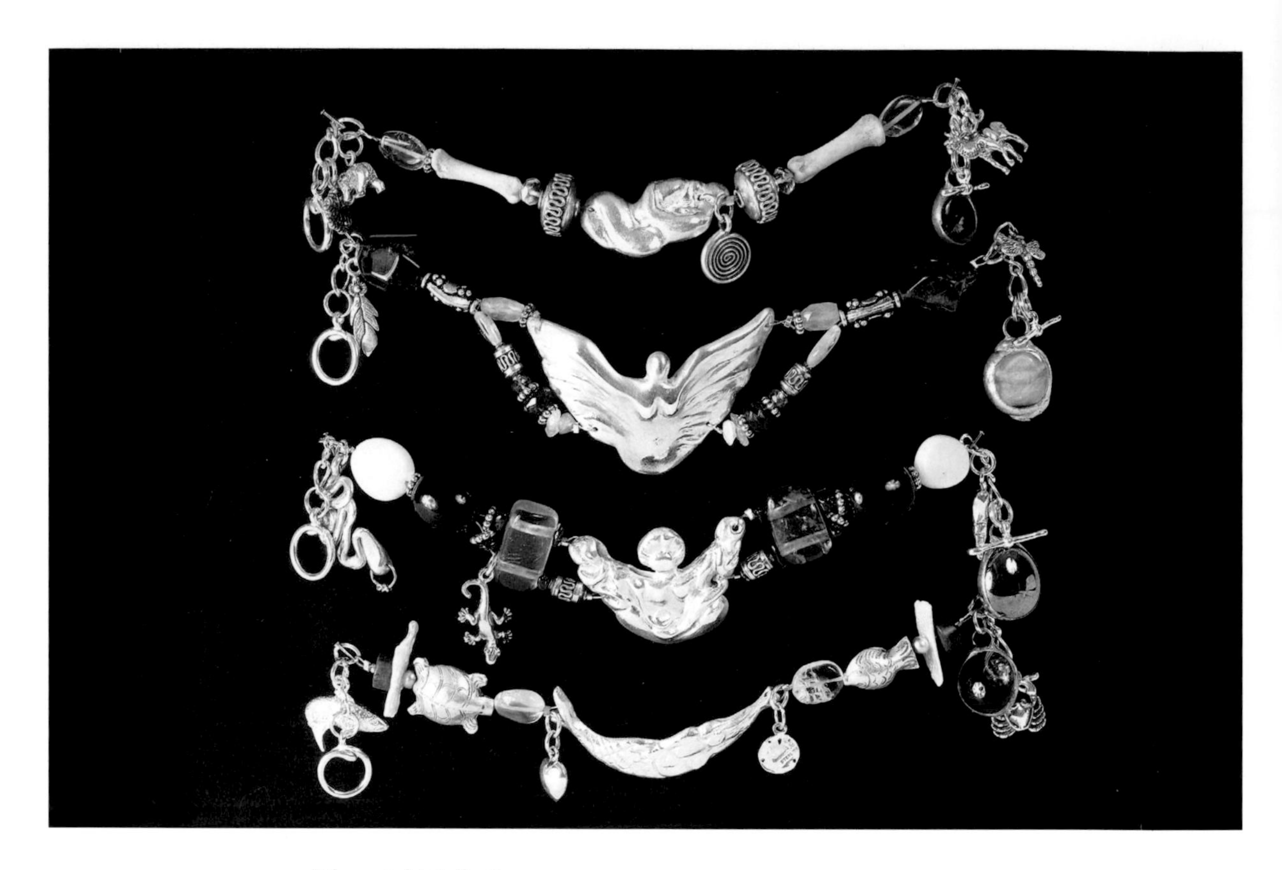

'Elementals' Collection
Bracelets: earth, air, fire and water, in fine silver with sterling silver charms and clasps, semi-precious stones

VERONICA STEWART journeyed through life and art mostly along the path of pottery before discovering a brilliant new product, Precious Metal Clay, or PMC, which is made up of three ingredients: silver, binder and water. After firing, the resulting silver clay can be handled and burnished like any other silver work. PMC opened up an entirely new direction for Veronica, enabling her to work in silver in much the same way as she worked in pottery clay, only on a smaller, more intricate scale. The *Elementals Jewelry* collection expresses her deep connection to the elements and to the ***community*** of women.

Veronica Stewart
Veronica Stewart Pottery and Design
250 595-0701
1561 Oakcrest Drive
Victoria, B.C. Canada V8P 1K7

'Elementals' Collection – Water
Necklace, bracelet and earrings in fine silver
with sterling silver charms and clasps,
semi-precious stones

LAURA BRYANT finds that her work in bodycasting demands a level of interaction with the subject that is rarely experienced by artists. Her contact with the formative materials: plaster and stone, lightweight cotton fibres and composite materials allows for a freedom of ***expression*** and a unique opportunity to design the final presentation of each piece. Marrying colour with the components helps bring each piece to life, particularly with the addition of light in its place of display. Her subject matter is the human form, of which Laura displays a true appreciation. She has exhibited in both Sooke and Victoria. While just a young woman in high school, she too worked at Sooke Harbour House.

Laura Bryant
Bodycasting Artform Studio
250 642-6645
2404 Mountain Heights
Sooke, B.C. Canada V0S 1N0

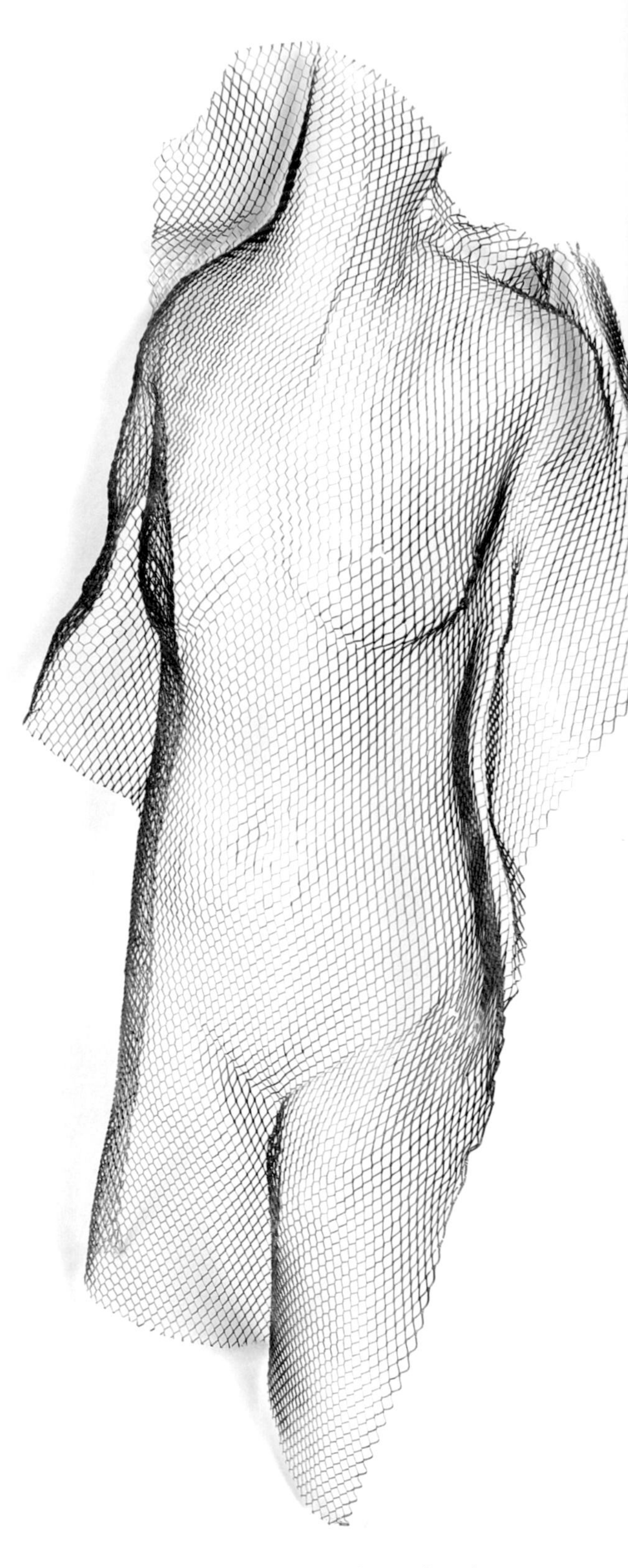

Wire Mesh Bodycasting
Wire mesh
Life-size

'Silent Siren' Mermaid
Acrylic and chalk pastels
on cotton fibre
Life-size
In collaboration with
Grania Bridal

Lavender Fields
Acrylic on board
8"w x 10"h

Coral Poser enjoys challenging herself by using fast-drying, acrylic paints. They urge her forward, into her creativity and out of managing expectations and maintaining control. This frees her spirit, opens her senses and makes her more available – to live her life and *evolve*. Coral has always loved to draw and paint, and as far back as she can remember has used her creativity to help make sense of the world. Coral's work has been featured in many solo exhibitions over the years in Nelson, Victoria and Vancouver. She also works as a Registered Massage Therapist in Sooke.

Coral Poser
250 642-0280
2151 Firwood Place
Sooke, B.C. V0S 1N0

Point No Point
Watercolour
7.5"w x 11"h

Whiffen Spit Driftwood
Watercolour
9.5"w x 6.5"h

Kananaskis Fields
Fiber art
46"w x 32.5"h

JOAN TAYLOR survived medical school, the raising of seven children and living on three continents before being able to concentrate on her art. With no formal art training, Joan exploits her ignorance of "the correct way" and just enjoys her own ***maverick*** process of discovery and creation. In the 1986 expansion of Sooke Harbour House, Joan made the ceramic tiles for the bathrooms, as well as for the Edible Flower room, the Beach Room and the Underwater Orchard Room.

After exploring a variety of media: watercolour, acrylics and china painting, Joan found working with fabrics, paint and threads to be the most fascinating of all creativities. She has exhibited at several Sooke Fine Arts exhibitions, and participated in group exhibitions in Australia.

Joan Taylor
250 646-2045
RR#7, 1037 Seaside Drive
Sooke, B.C. Canada V0S 1N0

Prairie Dreams
Fiber art
33"w x 26"h

Roasted Bosc Pears

with Minted Whipped Cream

Roasted Bosc Pears

Ingredients

3	Bosc pears, peeled, halved and cored
¾ cup	maple syrup
½ cup	unsalted butter, melted
2 tbsp	lemon thyme leaves

Method

1. Preheat oven to 350 degrees Fahrenheit.
2. Place the maple syrup, melted butter and the lemon thyme in a medium-sized bowl and whisk for one minute.
3. Add the pears and toss until they are well-coated.
4. Place the pears cut-side down in a 9 X 11 inch cake pan and pour the maple syrup mixture over top of them.
5. Bake for 35 to 45 minutes, flipping the pears every 10 minutes.
6. The pears are ready when a paring knife goes in and out of the fruit with very little resistance.
7. Remove the pears from the oven and let cool to room temperature.
8. Serve with minted whipped cream.

Minted Whipped Cream

Ingredients

½ cup	whipping cream
1 tbsp	honey
2 tbsp	finely chopped fresh mint

Method

1. Place all the ingredients in a small bowl and whip until the cream forms firm peaks.
2. Serve with maple syrup roasted pears.

Chef's Notes

Blue cheese and walnuts are delightful accompaniments to the roasted pears, and this dish is a great and impressive appetizer.

The pears can also be cut and put on a salad or pureed with apple juice to make a sauce.

To serve the roasted pears as dessert, try serving them with **Lavender Crème Brulée** (see page 80) or with chocolate or vanilla ice cream.

Margot Garwood
Golden Pears
Oil
24"w x 12"h

A Christmas Robin
Watercolour, Stochastic print,
limited edition of 500 s/n
9.5"w x 11"h

M. Morgan Warren was born in Great Britain and began her ***love*** affair with birds at a very early age. Personal knowledge and meticulous accuracy result in art full of charm and life. Among those collecting her paintings is HRH Prince Philip, Duke of Edinburgh. Morgan was also granted the rare privilege of making a personal gift of "*A Christmas Robin*" to Her Majesty, Queen Elizabeth II. As well, she was invited to demonstrate Audubon's techniques during the National Audubon Birds of America exhibition, at the De Young Museum of Fine Arts in San Francisco. Her work has appeared on the covers of many publications, including the international Sierra Club Foundation 1997 Annual Report. She is also recognized for her Save the Children Christmas cards (in '94/'95 and '95/'96), and a Ducks Unlimited print "*Winter Tapestry*". The waiting list for her original paintings is presently two years.

M. Morgan Warren
A-Frame Studio
250 655-1081 or 1 800 580-BIRD
Canoe Cove Marina
2300 Canoe Cove Road
North Saanich, B.C. Canada V8L 3X9

Autumn Bronze
Watercolour, lithograph,
limited edition of 300 s/n
14.875"w x 21"h

Great Blue
Watercolour, Giclée print,
limited edition of 50 s/n
14"w x 17"h

Pine Hutch in Garden Room
at Sooke Harbour House
7'6"w x 9'h

RUSTY AND ANN SAGE set up shop in Sooke over 20 years ago, crafting magnificent and often whimsical furniture pieces. Their work soon caught the eye of Frederique Philip and they began building furnishings for Sooke Harbour House. Over the years, they have created many unique pieces to compliment the various themes of different rooms, finding ***inspiration*** in the incredible natural beauty of the area. Their materials are locally grown woods: maple, yew, wild cherry and pine, often salvaged from logging operations. Rusty first learned the art of furniture construction while repairing antiques in his native England.

Rusty Sage
Sage Woodcrafters
250 642-3886
8982 West Coast Road
Sooke, B.C. Canada V0S 1N0

Pine and Paint Bed
in Emily Carr Room
at Sooke Harbour House
60"w x 60"h

Double Rocking Chair
Cherry Pine
44"w 40"h

TOM LAMONT developed his eye and feeling for wildlife when he worked in lookout towers as a Forest Service fire-spotter in northern British Columbia, Canada. His love and ***respect*** for animals is evident throughout his work. He carves moose antlers collected only from those that have dropped naturally from the live animal. Tom also works with individually selected pieces of soapstone from Brazil and alabaster from Spain. Each wildlife sculpture he creates is a combination of intimate study of the raw material, and an observed or envisioned pose of the animal. Tom welcomes custom orders; increasing demand has broadened the variety he offers.

Tom Lamont
Lamont's Art Gallery
250 752-8974
497 Corcan Road
Qualicum Beach, B.C. Canada V9K 2E9

Red-Eyed Tree Frog
Colorado alabaster and soapstone
151 lbs, 21"h

Sea Otters
Brazilian soapstone
80 lbs, 25"w

Baby Bear
Brazilian soapstone
40 lbs, 14"h

Edith, Victor and Carey Newman are a renowned artistic family. Carey opened the Blue Raven Gallery in 1996, not only to showcase his limited edition prints but also the prints and carvings of his father Victor, and the native fashion designs of his mother, Edith.

While most of Carey's creations are commissioned by private collectors, he has done work for corporations, government agencies and museums around the world. Of his 28 limited edition prints, 17 have sold out. He is also an accomplished musician in piano and voice and performs solo roles with Pacific Opera Victoria.

Of Kwagiulth and Salish descent, Victor Newman has a strong ***heritage*** in native art; his great-grandfather, Charlie James, was a master carver. Carey and Victor have started work on a totem pole for the waterfront garden of Sooke Harbour House. It will incorporate all the elements of the Philip family crest: sea gull, wild goose, jasmine flowers, cedar, wolf and whale. Victor's artwork can be found in private and public collections around the world.

An accomplished fibre artist and clothing designer, Edith Newman is of British heritage and does not feel comfortable creating the native designs for her clothing. Instead she explains her concept to her husband and son, who assist in interpreting her visions into native designs. Her work has been displayed in Italy, Paris and Toronto, and is in personal wardrobes world-wide. Edith's specialty is custom-designed clothing.

Please see page 17 for another image by Carey Newman, inspiration for the Bentwood Box Seaweed Broth *recipe.*

Edith, Victor and Carey Newman
Blue Raven Gallery
250 881-0528
1971 Kaltasin Road
Sooke, B.C. Canada V0S 1N0

Edith Newman
Blue Heron's Appliqued Evening Coat
Silk and doe suede
Model: Frederique Philip

Victor Newman
Moon
Carved and painted Alder mask
12"w x 14"h

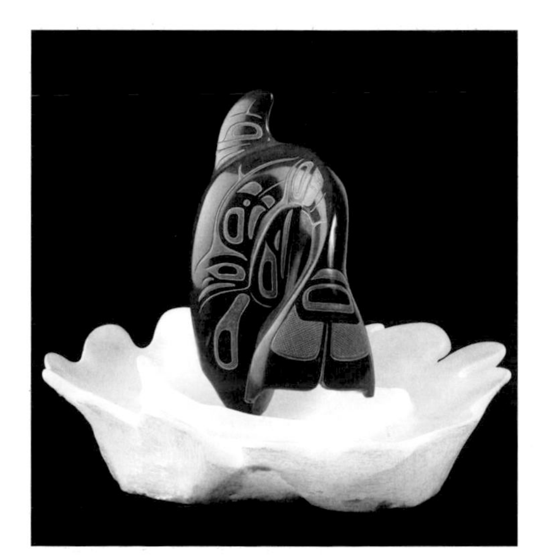

Carey Newman
Splash
Stone carving, peripholyte and alabaster
8.5"w x 6"d x 7"h

Honey Roasted Chicken

Stuffed with Garlic and Herbs

Ingredients

1	chicken, 4–5 lbs
2 tbsp	coarsely chopped rosemary
2 tbsp	coarsely chopped sage
2 tbsp	coarsely chopped oregano
20 cloves	garlic, whole, peeled
¼ cup	honey
2 tbsp	butter
½ tsp	salt
½ tsp	pepper

Method

1. Preheat the oven to 375 degrees Fahrenheit.
2. Place the garlic and herbs inside the chicken cavity.
3. Place the chicken in an oiled roasting pan and place in the oven.
4. In a small pot, melt the butter and add the honey, salt and pepper.
5. Remove the butter and honey glaze from the heat and whisk for one minute.
6. Baste the chicken with the honey glaze every 15 minutes.
7. Roast the chicken at 375 degrees for 15 minutes, then turn the oven down to 325 degrees and roast for another 45 minutes.
8. To test for doneness, insert a small knife into the leg between the inside of the thigh and the breast. When you remove the knife, the juice should run clear.
9. Pull the chicken from the oven, let rest for 10 minutes and serve.

Chef's Notes

For a slightly sweeter and somewhat more distinct taste, maple syrup can be substituted for the honey.

The roasted garlic can be served as a garnish, or pureed and turned into a flavourful sauce.

Cooked wild rice can be stuffed in the chicken for extra flavour and a more complete meal.

Other nice accompaniments are a salad or roasted vegetables.

This chicken also turns out great when cooked on a rotisserie or on a barbeque.

"When I saw the rooster in wrought iron, I immediately thought
of a spit-roasted rooster or chicken.
But it's not that easy to do a spit-roasted rooster so,
(for the purposes of this book),

Nancy Powell
Black Cat Forge
Mr. White's Cock
Hot forged steel
33"w x 40"h

I did a whole roasted chicken stuffed with garlic.
It was simple, but it's good, really good."

Edward Tuson

Ikebana Flowers Basket
Ceramic with metallic glaze
6"w x 9.5"h

SUE HARA believes in living *and* working creatively, undertaking every task with an artist's eye. She works from a place of ***spirit***, seeing her ceramic pieces as soul food rather than just "things" in a materialistic culture. She began by making both functional and decorative pieces, using many techniques. Now Sue is fusing her two loves, pottery and gardening, and creating garden art (birdbaths) and flower containers suitable for Ikebana. Sue has exhibited across the country. Her work can be found in the collections of the Bronfman Corporation, the Winnipeg Art Gallery and the Maltwood Gallery, University of Victoria.

Sue Hara
250 385-9029
1245 Queens Avenue
Victoria, B.C. Canada V8T 1N1

Ikebana Vase with Handle
Ceramic
3.5"w x 18"h

Birdbath with Birds
Ceramic, frostproof
10"w x 12"h

Rock Cod
Port Renfrew Marble
175 lbs, 27"w x 12"d x 14"h

GARY PEARSON served for 20 years in the Canadian Navy and worked as a commercial Rock cod fisher for seven years, supplying live fish to Victoria's Undersea Gardens and occasionally to the Vancouver Public Aquarium. On his way into Victoria to make his deliveries, he would drop off fresh rockfish at Sooke Harbour House, for its daily menu. Understandably then, his subjects are of the sea, strongly sculpted in *local* marble, from veins that Gary and his wife Karen discovered. Gary is a member of the West Coast Sculpture Association and has participated in the Victoria Natural History Society Art Show.

RIGHT
Rare Vancouver Island Marble deposit in Port Renfrew
This large body of marble was formed from shells 320 million years ago, when Vancouver Island, Queen Charlotte Island and the south end of Alaska were all one undersea volcanic terrain near the equator. The deposit may contain decorative stone that exists nowhere else in North America.

Gary Pearson
250 647-5460
70 Wickaninnish Road
Port Renfrew, B.C. Canada V0S 1K0

Blue Salmon
Port Renfrew Marble
22"w x 4"d x 10"h

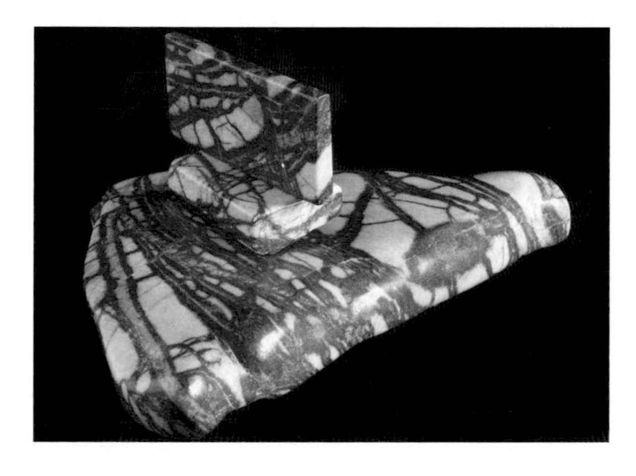

Three pieces of Orca marble
10"w x 9"d x 1.5"h
(Display only)

Frank Armich was born on Vancouver Island. As a young apprentice in his father's business of producing burl wood furniture and clocks, Frank quickly developed a keen attraction to the inherent ***beauty*** of local woods: Bird's Eye Maple, Red and Yellow Cedar, Fir. Today he creates by hand an extensive line of artistic sculptures such as mirrors, mystical trees, bowls, whales and wall pieces, out of these woods. Frank also uses a variety of roots to create one-of-a-kind chairs, tables, lamps and beds...and houses built out of driftwood. In addition, he enjoys crafting silver-plated, whimsical wind chimes. He has exhibited across Vancouver Island and throughout North America.

Frank Armich
Frankly Yours Unique Woodworking and Wind Chimes
250 248-2900
222 James Street
Parksville, B.C. Canada V9P 1H9

Diamond Willow Wonder
Fir burl base with
Bird's Eye Maple top
8'4"h

Red Cedar burl mirror
28"w x 22"h

Curly Maple tree
7"w x 33"h

Red Cedar burl bowl
12.5"w x 5.5"h

The Runner
Fir root sculpture
mounted on
a Red Cedar burl
11"w x 18"h

Sun Mask
Yellow Cedar
49"w x 51"h

ALLAN BLYTH educated his eye in the techniques and *craftsmanship* of carving at a very early age. Born and raised in Victoria, British Columbia, he spent hours as a child watching master carvers restore ancient totem poles and house-posts destined for the Victoria Museum. In his 20s, Al was introduced to a master carver who became his teacher in the Kwagiulth style. He carved and painted as a hobby for many years, earning his living in the shipyards and the family business. When an industrial accident cut his career short, Al began carving full-time. He creates ceremonial masks, as well as bowls, boxes, walking sticks and feast dishes. Soon he will be incorporating metal casting, stone, bone, and other natural materials, in his works.

Allan Blyth
250 749-4696
Box 281
Lake Cowichan, B.C. Canada V0R 2G0

'Pugwis' Sea Monster
Wood/Cedar bark
Mask: 15w x 24"h
With 'hair': 54"h

Herbal Tea Spritzer

Ingredients

½ cup	Sooke Harbour House Sweet Lemon Tea or Mint Blend
5 cups	boiling water
1 cup	cranberry juice
2 cups	soda water
2 cups	sparkling Elderflower water

Method

1. Steep the tea for five to seven minutes, pour into a pitcher and refrigerate for one hour.
2. Add all remaining ingredients and refrigerate for an additional half hour.
3. Serve over ice with a fresh mint, lemon balm, fennel or sweet cicely garnish.

Chef's Notes

If the Sooke Harbour House teas are unavailable, use your favourite tea instead.

For a more attractive drink, make frozen herb ice cubes and use instead of normal ice.

Sweeten with maple syrup or honey.

For a thicker and delicious drink, add a little bit of condensed milk.

"Nishka's teapot inspired
the herbal tea recipe,
which I turned into a Spritzer."

Edward Tuson

Nishka Philip

Teapots

Intaglio colour prints

10"w x 10"h

Pitcher Still Life
Watercolour on canvas
12"w x 12"h

Margot Garwood is best known for her ***luminous*** watercolour paintings but also works in oil, charcoal and collage. In addition to her formal education at the University of Alberta, she has also studied at the Victoria College of Art. A member of the Warrior Women Artists' Collective and the Community Arts Council of Greater Victoria, her work is shown throughout the city. During summer weekends, she exhibits, paints and sells her works in the Bastion Square Festival of the Arts. Margot's paintings can be found in private collections around the world.

Please see page 111 for another image by Margot Garwood, inspiration for the recipe Roasted Bosc Pears with Minted Whipped Cream.

Margot Garwood
250 598-1082
2756 Belmont Avenue
Victoria, B.C. Canada V8R 4A8

Kitchen Shelf
Watercolour
5"w x 12"h

PAULINE OLESEN lives on a small West Coast island, where the sea and her garden continuously instill themselves in her glass works. Self-taught in all areas, Pauline first worked in hand-painted tiles, ceramics and pottery, which led to firing glass into carved clay forms. This carried on to fusing. Along the way, Pauline discovered she loves the transformative process of firing, and glasswork has now become her focus. She finds every work to be part *experiment* because the final outcome, the opening of the kiln, is always a surprise that has yet to disappoint.

Pauline Olesen
250 655-4812
123 McKenzie Crescent
Piers Island, B.C. Canada V8L 5Y7

Painted Canyon
Fused glass with aluminum stand
9"w x 11"h

Purple Abstract Bowl
Fused glass
11.5" diameter

Purple Iris
Fused glass
9"w x 14"h

Hot Pot series
Gouache/ink
2.5"w x 4.5"h

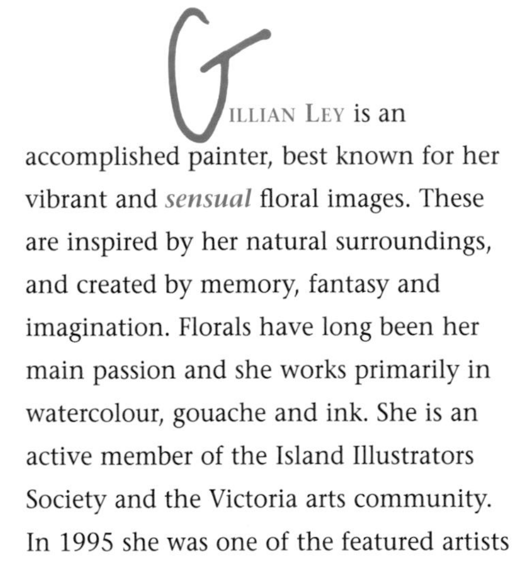

Gillian Ley is an accomplished painter, best known for her vibrant and *sensual* floral images. These are inspired by her natural surroundings, and created by memory, fantasy and imagination. Florals have long been her main passion and she works primarily in watercolour, gouache and ink. She is an active member of the Island Illustrators Society and the Victoria arts community. In 1995 she was one of the featured artists at the Royal British Columbia Museum Illustrators Showcase. Gillian teaches painting classes through the University of Victoria's Extension Programs, and also works as a successful residential and commercial Interior Designer.

Please see pages 43 and 141 for other images by Gillian Ley, inspiration for the recipes Arugula Dianthus Salad with a Rose Petal Vinaigrette *and* Seared Scallops Salad with Pickled Daikon Radish.

Gillian Ley
250 383-3090
4-423 Kingston Street
Victoria, B.C. Canada V8V 1V8

Hot Pot series
Gouache/ink
2.5"w x 4.5"h

Blue Tea (Pot Belly series)
Raku
6"w x 13"h

ANGELA MONTANTI'S passion is ceramics, particularly raku. While her work ranges from the sculptural to the decorative to the functional, most of her work is decorative and is imbued with humour and *whimsy*. Each piece combines a collection of images, shapes and colours in a seemingly functional form. As part of her creative process, Angela imagines her work in public or personal spaces, studied and viewed through imagination and interpretation. A graduate of the University of Manitoba with a BFA Honours, Angela admits to an 'obsession' with raku that continues to be a constant stimulus to her work.

Angela Montanti
250 655-9188
1727 Lopez Place
Sidney, B.C. Canada V8L 4X5

Fishing Boat
Raku
11"w x 13"h

Dark City Tea Pot
Raku
11"w x 16"h

Arugula and Dianthus Salad

with a Rose Petal Vinaigrette

Arugula Dianthus Salad

Wash, pat dry and toss the following in a medium-sized bowl:

½ cup	Dianthus flower petals
2 cups	Arugula

Crispy Daylily Flowers

Ingredients

1	egg white
2 tsp	baking powder
½ cup	cornstarch
½ cup	corn meal
¾ cup	milk
½ tsp	salt
½ tsp	pepper
3 cups	safflower oil, for frying
6	Daylily flowers, pistils removed

Method

1. Place all dry ingredients except the flowers in one small bowl and all wet ingredients except the oil in a separate small bowl. Mix each well.
2. Whisk the wet ingredients into the dry, until the two form a smooth, uniform batter and then refrigerate.
3. Place the safflower oil in a small, one-quart pot and heat to 325 degrees Fahrenheit.
4. Dip the whole Daylily flower in the batter and deep fry for two to three minutes.
5. Place the deep-fried flower on a paper towel and let cool for one minute.
6. The Daylily flowers may be deep fried two at a time.

Rose Petal Vinaigrette

Ingredients

2 cups	Wild Rose petals
¾ cup	apple juice
½ cup	white wine vinegar
2 tsp	honey

Method:

1. Place all ingredients except the rose petals in a small pot and bring to a boil.
2. Place the rose petals in a jar, and pour the hot vinaigrette over them. Cover, let cool and refrigerate for six hours.

Johnny Jump Up Oil

Ingredients

½ cup	Johnny Jump Ups or Pansies with stems
½ cup	safflower oil

Method:

1. Place flowers and oil in a high-speed blender and blend on high speed for two minutes.
2. Pour oil into a jar with a lid, cover and refrigerate for a minimum of one hour.

Presentation of the Dish

1. In a small bowl, place three tablespoons of the Johnny Jump Up oil and two tablespoons of the Rose Petal vinegar.
2. Pour the vinaigrette over the Arugula and Dianthus flower salad.
3. Toss the salad in the vinaigrette and serve among six plates.
4. Place a crispy Daylily flower atop each salad plate.

Gillian Ley
Tossed
Gouache/watercolour
12"w x 13"h

Chef's Notes

Prepare the salad and the dressing before frying the Daylily flowers.

Arugula and Dianthus flower would be tasty on a shrimp sandwich.

Rose petal vinaigrette is also very nice served with fish.

Crispy Daylily flower would be a good garnish for the baked **Sole-wrapped Lingcod** (see page 34).

"Gillian's laced flowers inspired a salad using only those ingredients, with a crispy Daylily flower, a vinaigrette made from the rose and the pansies and then the salad made from the Arugula and Dianthus."

Edward Tuson

Sea Monster
Red Cedar mask,
cedar bark and
acrylic paint
Mask: 12"w x 20"h
With 'hair': 48"h

Derek Heaton creates a contemporary version of a very old coastal Indian art form learned from Willie Seaweeds, a Kwagiulth Master Carver. Born of Mikmak and Chinese heritage, Derek sought and received permission to study and work in this art form. *Reverence* for the work stems from his belief that his ability to create is a gift from the creator. In order to more fully express what he sees and feels, he intends to venture into other media: stone, metal and exotic woods. Derek's hope for his art is that it will touch people in a positive way

Derek Heaton
250 479-8974
4901 B East Sooke Road
Sooke, B.C. Canada V0S 1N0

Crooked Beak of Heaven
Red Cedar, cedar bark and acrylic paint;
skirt of Red Cedar bark and copper
Mask: 9"w x 36"d x 36"h
With skirt: 46"h

Misty Blue
Watercolour
7"w x 19"h

Judi Wild first employed her artistic talent as a draftsperson, and then as a graphic artist. After more than 20 years in the corporate world, she turned to painting, developing and mastering the ***labour-intensive*** method of applying watercolours using the 'drybrush' technique. This gives her work that extra dimension in the delicate detailing she painstakingly portrays. Judi taught her unusual painting style for some time but is now consumed by her work. She is represented in the National Archives of Canada and in many corporate collections world-wide. She has won several competitions including the "Peoples Choice" award in 1996 and again in 1998 at the Parksville/Qualicum Brant Festival on Vancouver Island.

Judi Wild
250 335-1151
RR#1, Site 37, C29
Fanny Bay, B.C. Canada V0R 1W0

Spirit of Chief Ninstints
Watercolour
17.5"w x 37.75"h

Guardian of the Spirit Bear
Watercolour
26"w x 36"h

JACK WILLOUGHBY'S unique ironwork sells out at international garden shows and can be found in art galleries, gift shops and private homes throughout North America, Europe and Japan. The strength and ***simplicity*** of his work shows well in the home or outside in the garden. Born in Newport News, Virginia, Jack spent part of his youth in California before moving to Vancouver Island, where the ocean beaches inspire his work. His career as an artist began in steel working, then teaching metal work at a Vancouver college. There, with the freedom to create his own designs, he discovered a wealth of talent that soon compelled him to become a full-time artist.

Stone and Steel Duck
Stone and Steel
3"w x 4.5"h
(Available in different sizes.)

Jack Willoughby
Anvil Island Design
250 751-1160
1920 Wilfert Road
Nanaimo, B.C. Canada V9S 3H5

Blue Heron
Steel
5.5"w x 12"h
(Available in different sizes.)

Dancing Ladies
Steel
22"w x 5"h

In his own words:

RENAAT MARCHAND 29 March 1962
Born in Belgium, Lokeren
Married to Krista and father of Arno and Dana
Taught art and woodworking
Moved away from busy Belgium in April, 2000
Thought I'd move closer to ***Paradise***.

Worked in boat-building and construction to experience the Canadian way
No time to waste.

No longer worker ant, adding value to this wonderful coastline.
Woodworker with enormous respect for our trees,
I admire them and all creatures.
Thankful that I'm able to use these materials that I'm hoping
to replace in my lifespan.

Renaat Marchand
250 642-7827
7827 Dalrae Place
Sooke, B.C. Canada V0S 1N0

Ocean Sculpture Fence
Split cedar, copper and glass
46'w x 6'h

Carved Salmon
Cedar
32'w

Pick up the broken pieces and create a new nature, a new life,
Never as perfect as the irreplaceable.
Express anger, fear. My good nature, my beliefs.

What can we do for all this beauty?
Happy ant in my new world.
Renaissance, born again.

Enjoy.

Art and Economic Benefit

JUST AS ART, and the understanding of its benefits, have been essential ingredients in the success of Sooke Harbour House, so art has been fundamental to the revitalization of the Vancouver Island town of Chemainus. This artful community of about 3900 souls is an hour's drive north of the city of Victoria. It presently boasts 33 dramatic outdoor murals that depict the town's history, its people and environs. Just as intended, the murals have become a major tourist attraction; Chemainus now hosts 400,000 visitors annually. Prior to the painting of the first five murals in 1982, Chemainus attracted no visitors at all.

"In fact, our population back then was considerably less," says Karl Schutz, resident and originator of the mural project, "so if you saw a stranger in Chemainus in the late '70s, you knew they were lost!"

A mill town for 150 years, Chemainus started to decline in the early 1980s and the mill closed in 1983. Karl, Project Coordinator for revitalization of downtown Chemainus, proposed the mural project as part of that revitalization. The Mayor at the time, 27-year old Graham Bruce, sold the mural idea to the townsfolk, on a trial basis. Five murals were painted initially, and they started working their magic immediately. Within two hours of the first brushstroke, people stopped by to see the artwork...and word of mouth started. Seven more murals were painted in 1983, more people stopped by, and 'the rest is history.' Since then over 40 artists from Canada, Scotland and the U.S.A. have collaborated on the Chemainus murals.

West Coast Renaissance

The success of Chemainus gave birth to the **Arts and Cultural Accord Foundation**, which is a coalition of artists, arts organizations, commerce, tourism and government leaders, to promote and develop the arts as an industry on Vancouver Island, the Gulf Islands and the Sunshine Coast of British Columbia.

"Just imagine this," prompts Karl, "arts and tourism being the number one industry in British Columbia! That's our vision."

Native Heritage
Mural
50.53'w x 20.34'h

He adds, "Art can generate a totally new economy; it has already been proven in Chemainus. From a sawmill town to a town of art murals, theatre and performing arts...it's such a huge gap to have bridged. Here we have a role model for everyone to follow.

"We realize that the murals were only the foundation for the new arts and cultural industry for our town. And now there are over 100 communities in North America that are utilizing art and culture to provide new economic life," Karl declares.

The Arts and Cultural Accord Foundation entered its fifth year in 2003, with dozens of projects in development. One of them, the Arts and Cultural Highway, is a self-guided, circle tour of the art and cultural resources of the Gulf Islands, Vancouver Island and the Sunshine Coast. Another continuous, 'work in progress' is the building of an on-line portal to those same resources, with related links, at www.gobc.ca.

Funding for all this is based on the Magic Chemainus Financial Success Formula, "whereby every stakeholder invests a little and everyone wins a lot," Karl explains. He adds, "The Foundation is still in its infancy. Our vision and its success are only limited by our imaginations."

Karl Schutz
Photo by
Neil Newton

PUTTING A FACE TO THE NAME

Frank Armich
Page 126

Sheila Beech
Page 76

Craig Benson
Page 84

Anne Boquist
Page 60

Laura Bryant
Page 104

Linda Danielson
Page 22

Dennis Demarchi
Page 28

Michel Des Rochers
Page 98

Simon Des Rochers
Page 50

Dulcie Draper
Page 18

Susan Elkins
Page 30

d.a. farley
Page 74

Andrei Fedorov
Photographer

Margot Garwood
Page 132

Dinah Giffin
Page 66

Kerry Gortan
Page 38

Paul Grignon
Page 56

Sue Hara
Page 122

Wally Head
Page 54

Derek Heaton
Page 142

Keith Hiscock
Page 82

Susan Isaac
Page 68

Will Julsing
Page 20

Kimiko
Page 40

Tom Lamont
Page 116

Gillian Ley
Page 136

Aivars Logins
Page 70

Jan Lovewell
Page 88

Renaat Marchand
Page 148

Glenys Marshall-Inman
Page 44

Robert Martin
Page 36

Alice McLean
Page 32

Lori Messer
Page 26

Norra Mirosevic
Page 46

Angela Montanti
Page 138

Edith Newman
Page 118

Victor Newman
Page 118

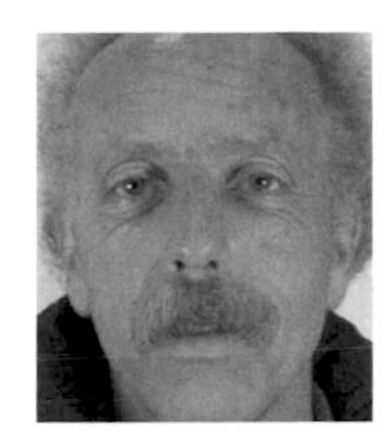

Kim Nilson
Page 94

Pauline Olesen
Page 134

Gary Pearson
Page 124

Jasmine Philip
Lettering artist

Nishka Philip
Page 96

Coral Poser
Page 106

Nancy Powell
Page 58

Rintje Raap
Page 92

Christine Reimer
Page 64

Ron Robb
Page 88

Rusty Sage
Page 114

Veronica Stewart
Page 102

Joan Taylor
Page 108

Sandy Sydnam
Page 48

Dennis Shields
Page 78

M. Morgan Warren
Page 112

Judi Wild
Page 144

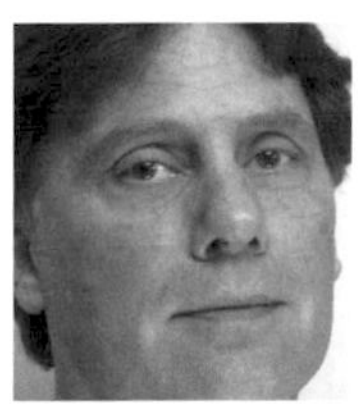

Marn Williams
Page 68

Jack Willoughby
Page 146

THE ART OF SOOKE HARBOUR HOUSE

has been typeset

in the Stone Serif and Legacy Sans type families.

Lettering art for heads and initial capital letters

is by Jasmine Philip.

This is a British Columbia book,

from concept, writing, design and production,

to pre-press and printing.

The paper used for its cover and pages is Luna Silk,

a coated stock manufactured on Annacis Island, British Columbia.